Uncle Sam Presents

Well, Joe, looks like we've got another hit on our hands.

Uncle Sam
Presents

A Memoir of the Federal Theatre
1935–1939

TONY BUTTITTA
and BARRY WITHAM

With drawings by
DON FREEMAN

The University of Pennsylvania Press
Philadelphia · 1982

Dream of the Lost Colony on p. 172 is published with
the approval of the Roanoke Island Historical Association, Inc., owner of the text of The Lost Colony.

The photo of Eleanor Roosevelt on p. 173 is published
courtesy of the Roanoke Island Historical Association.

Drawings by Don Freeman appear on the following
pages: ii, 9, 46, 59, 62, 75, 85, 86, 137, 142, 159, and 182.

Photos appearing on pp. 13, 34, and 43 are reprinted
with permission of the Library of Congress Federal
Theatre Project Collection at George Mason University Libraries, Fairfax, Virginia.

The photo on p. 162 is by Aycock Brown. Courtesy of
Mrs. Paul Green.

This work was published with the support of the
Haney Foundation.

Library of Congress Cataloging in Publication Data

Buttitta, Tony.
  Uncle Sam presents.

  Bibliography: p.
  Includes index.
  1. Federal Theatre Project (U.S.) I. Witham,
Barry, 1939-   II. Title.
PN2270.F43B8   792'.0973   81-43517
ISBN 0-8122-7826-7   AACR2

Printed in the United States of America

Contents

Abbreviations

AAA	Agricultural Adjustment Act
CCC	Civilian Conservation Corps
CWA	Civil Works Administration
ERA	Emergency Relief Act
FERA	Federal Emergency Relief Administration
NRA	National Recovery Administration
WPA	Works Progress Administration
PWA	Public Works Administration

Foreword

by Malcolm Cowley

AMONG all the experiments undertaken by the New Deal, it is the Federal Theatre Project that seems in retrospect to be the most picturesque and, in its own terms, the most remarkable. It began as a relief measure, one designed to create jobs in their own field, at subsistence wages, for ten thousand theatre people who were suffering more than others from lack of demand for their services. In that bleak year 1935, who could afford to buy tickets for a Broadway show? Hallie Flanagan, the gifted director of the project, thought she could find work for unemployed actors and entertainers at minimum expense to the Federal Government, but she had grander aims as well. She wanted to create a new theatre closer to American realities, even as she wanted to give scope to new talents and to make stage performances available at a low admission price, or none at all, to millions of Americans who had never seen a live actor.

"Bread and circuses," her enemies said, and Congress was full of these. The enemies triumphed in 1939, when Congress put an end to the Federal Theatre after only four years, but its achievements were too vital to be forgotten. Some of the new talents Hallie Flanagan encouraged went on to famous careers on stage or screen (John Houseman and Orson Welles among many others). The new methods they introduced helped to transform the American stage.

Mrs. Flanagan has told the story of the project in her book *Arena* (1940), writing (and writing well) from her own standpoint as its director engaged in a hopeless battle with Congress. Tony Buttitta, in the present volume, tells a more intimate story of what it meant to work on the project from day to day, first as a reporter for *The Federal Theatre Magazine*, then as press agent for several productions (including a fa-

Foreword

mous one, Marc Blitzstein's *The Cradle Will Rock* [which was canceled]). Thus, he had an overview of events, and an underview as well. He was chiefly a distant spectator of the struggle in Washington, but in New York Tony was part of the action: he argued, he took notes, and he vividly remembers. Personalities, quarrels, crises, parades up Broadway, victories with the public, and falsehoods in the press: his book records all these in a firsthand narrative that brings back to life a tumultuous and fruitful era for the American stage.

Introduction

by Harold Clurman

THERE is much talk nowadays about experimental theatre. It relates to methods intended to expand the techniques and styles of the traditional theatre. The "movement" is important but still only a côterie manifestation. The most truly experimental effort ever undertaken in the American theatre is the subject of this book: the Federal Theatre established under the Works Progress Administration from 1935 to 1939.

It was experimental nationwide and artistically, even as it was committed to administrative and technical innovation. Its personnel was the largest ever engaged at one and the same time in the American theatre. It offered the widest repertoire (in many different languages), and discovered a host of new personalities who were to make signal contributions to our stage. In its specific accomplishments and in its symbolic significance for the future it was one of the most portentous phenomena in the cultural pursuit of our land.

Most Americans are insufficiently familiar with their country's theatre history. One of the remarkable aspects of this memoir by an active participant in the chronicled events is that it is not solely theatre history but *American* history as well and its cast of characters are personally seen in their action and reaction to the broad scene of their day.

The thirties were stirring times. They are usually referred to as the era of the great Depression. But I call them *the fervent years.* The fifteen million unemployed, the evictions, the breadlines, the "Hoovervilles" (hovels set up by the homeless) produced a panorama of despair, but most heartening as well as amazing was the fortitude with which it was faced. The Works Progress Administration, and, as part of it, the Federal Theatre, was our government's response to this crisis.

Introduction

At the head of the Federal Theatre was a diminutive college professor of great courage: Hallie Flanagan. She was more indefatigable and intrepid than any other person who has ever entered the lists of combat or good works in the arena of our entertainment world.

Under her leadership and that of her many notable collaborators, unknown craftsmen and artists rose to fame through contributions of lasting effect. There was the prodigious Orson Welles, the wide-ranging producer John Houseman, the film directors Sidney Lumet, Joe Losey, the playwrights Paul Green, Mary Chase, Sinclair Lewis—whose one successful play, *It Can't Happen Here,* was written for the Federal Theatre—the composers Marc Blitzstein, Paul Bowles, and Virgil Thomson, the dancers Tamiris and Edwin Denby—later an outstanding dance critic—the actors Joseph Cotten, Canada Lee, Will Geer, the conductor-composer Lehman Engel, the puppeteer Remo Bufano, the costume designer Irene Sharaff: a complete list would cover pages.

T.S. Eliot's historical verse play, *Murder in the Cathedral,* was a tremendous success (at very low prices as were all the Federal Theatre offerings). When this play was later produced on Broadway, it failed because Broadway did not attract a truly *popular,* or broadly based, audience. The Federal Theatre audience was composed of the young (who rarely attended the commercial theatre), the old and many, many throughout the land who had never had the opportunity or the cash to see any sort of "living theatre." Also included in the roster of Federal Theatre productions, a Hallie Flanagan favorite, was a circus. And the response of these new, fresh audiences—who must certainly have been moviegoers as well—was positively exuberant.

The audiences did not simply become acquainted with drama—Shakespeare and Marlowe as well as contemporaries—but were brought in touch with the world. (Isn't that what theatre is for?) Abroad, German, Italian, and Spanish fascism loomed ominously, but large segments of our people were only faintly conscious of its dangerous presence. The

Introduction

Federal Theatre performances brought enlightenment in this matter as they did on many of the government's programs in the agricultural, industrial, and scientific fields. What our black citizens (not to mention other minority groups) could contribute to the arts was revealed in numerous productions (the Welles-Houseman *Macbeth* in Harlem, for instance) to the immense delight of the general public.

These things and much more of the vast spectacle are vividly brought to our attention in this book. But in respect to theatre history alone, perhaps the outstanding contribution was the creation of a novel stage form: the Living Newspaper, which dramatized in short, swift-moving scenes problems of modern social life and methods of dealing with them. The most sensationally acclaimed of the living newspapers was *One Third of a Nation,* the epic play which traced the struggle for proper housing in New York from 1705 to 1938.

The story of the Federal Theatre is itself epical. It impinges on government, on politics and politicians (in this regard, a veritable melodrama!), and if it had no other value, it should serve as a lesson, an inspiration, and an incentive to the youth of today. It is a story that needs to be told and bears repetition. It leads to an urge to practical emulation.

I speak of a lesson that may be stated in this memoir and in Hallie Flanagan's own reverberant words: ". . . a national theatre must have government subsidy because its scope [is] beyond that of private enterprise. Federal Theatre learned that the government could put on shows as well as any legitimate producer. It also learned something more important— millions of Americans wanted to go to the theatre if it could be brought 'geographically and financially within their range. These public theatres explored sources of native American life and used this material in regional American drama.' "

"But if the government," Flanagan adds, "is concerned with making its people better citizens and individuals, then it should concern itself more and more with theatre. Not theatre as a luxury, but as a necessity."

xv

ACT ONE

Hanging the Show
August 27, 1935

1

ON a cool summer morning in 1935, in the mountain town of Asheville, North Carolina, I read that Hallie Flanagan had been named national director of the Federal Theatre Project. The news that Uncle Sam was going into show business intrigued me. Although I was a busy young man trying to make ends meet as a freelance reporter, bookseller, and press agent for the state-supported North Carolina Symphony Orchestra, I was ready to drop everything to take my chances with this venture.

The Federal Theatre was one of the four Arts projects set up late that summer under the Works Progress Administration (WPA) as a work relief program to employ thousands of jobless writers, artists, musicians, actors, and others in the theatre. I approved of the kind of theatre that Hallie Flanagan hoped to establish: a theatre born out of economic necessity, not art theory, and concerned with the changing social order.

Busy as she was setting up the national project, I was confident that Flanagan would remember me. I had known her since 1931, when her documentary drama *Can You Hear Their Voices?* attracted national attention to Vassar where she directed the Experimental Theatre. Colleges and community theatres, as well as union and workers' groups, had produced the socially significant play everywhere and raised funds to help the Arkansas drought victims depicted in it.

Flanagan had known *Contempo,* the controversial little magazine which I had edited at Chapel Hill and which had drawn its own share of national attention with our issues on Scottsboro, Shaw, and Faulkner. She also knew about my association with playwright Paul Green and Professor Frederick Koch, founder of the Carolina Playmakers, who had produced an experimental play which I wrote while I was a graduate student at the University of North Carolina. Along

3

with other prominent theatre people, Green and Koch had advised Flanagan at the time she was drafting plans for the project, which were to be presented to Harry Hopkins, WPA national administrator.

Hopkins, a fellow Iowan, had chosen Flanagan to head the project on the strength of her work at Vassar and her Guggenheim-sponsored study of private and state-supported theatres in Europe and the Soviet Union. Her background was also familiar to President Roosevelt, a Vassar trustee, and to Eleanor Roosevelt, who was behind the scenes during the planning and was keeping a motherly eye on the operation of the four Arts projects, known as Federal One.

They considered Flanagan the ideal choice to direct the theatre project, aimed as it was toward making jobs rather than profits and helping the ailing theatre industry recover from the combined assault of motion pictures, radio, and the Depression. At the time Flanagan was a stranger to the Broadway clique whose main interest was in commercial plays and musicals, described by showman Billy Rose as "satin and lumber." This was to her credit, however, since President Roosevelt wanted no one from that background as national director of the project.

A firm believer in the social function of the theatre, along with its necessary function as entertainment, Flanagan wanted to stage plays in an experimental way, since she was more interested in new techniques and a fresh approach than money. The plays she chose appealed to a much wider audience than the vanishing carriage trade that considered itself the patron and mainstay of the legitimate theatre.

In October Hallie wired me that she was planning a *Federal Theatre Magazine,* which was to be published in New York and asked whether I would help edit it. I promptly let her know I was interested. Encouraged by her reply, I hung out a *For Sale* sign in the small bookshop I was running in a downtown hotel and began negotiating with an Asheville *Citizen-Times* reporter who saw the business as a possible outlet for his wife's excess energy.

A short time later Hallie wrote that WPA red tape made it almost impossible to engage anyone from one state to work in another. But she was still trying. She also mentioned that they had obtained a small multilith offset press from the Rockefeller Foundation to print the magazine. Several weeks passed. I read of troubles in Chicago and New York with the initial editions of the Living Newspaper, the experimental unit set up to dramatize pertinent news events in a novel theatrical form, partly inspired by *Can You Hear Their Voices?*

The Chicago unit was preparing a production on slum conditions and New York was researching and writing about Mussolini's rape of Ethiopia. Flanagan and Elmer Rice, the New York City project director, knew that the subjects were controversial and might have political repercussions, but they felt that the Federal Theatre could present them as stage documentaries. And they had Harry Hopkins' assurance that they were running the show and that their efforts would be "free, adult, and uncensored."

Then, within the same week in January 1936, both productions were shelved before their scheduled opening dates. The Mayor of Chicago, a local boss who belonged to the Democratic machine which had backed Roosevelt, was behind the scenes to close the first, *Model Tenement.* The State Department, fearing that *Ethiopia* might offend Mussolini, discussed changes with Flanagan which she did not find unreasonable. But Rice resigned amidst charges of censorship that made headlines across the nation. *Ethiopia* was shut down and Flanagan faced a shaky project and the job of bolstering the morale of her regional directors before a single curtain had gone up on a major Federal Theatre production.

This news came to me from newspapers and mimeographed issues of the Federal Theatre *Bulletin,* which summarized project activities in a chatty house-organ style. I was pleased to note in the *Bulletin* that dozens of other productions were announced or in rehearsal. New York and Los Angeles were vying to see who would open first. Both had classical units and personnel inherited from earlier state and federal programs. Los Angeles was preparing *The Knight of the Burning Pestle* at a university theatre; New York, a Shakespeare comedy for spot bookings in the five boroughs. With all the initial chaos, miscues and crises, Flanagan found it more symbolic than appropriate that the first Federal Theatre show to ring up a curtain was *The Comedy of Errors* on January 13, 1936.

Two of my friends were not in favor of my leaving Asheville. One was Lamar Stringfield, the composer and symphony conductor who had hired me that spring as a press agent. I had already learned enough about that craft to dislike it, but Stringfield insisted that I was being unfair to leave him now that I was finally becoming of some value. He kept on about it until one day in February he handed me an official memo calling for cuts in his personnel, orchestra reorganization, and the dropping of all non-musicians. The other was F. Scott Fitzgerald, who came to the bookshop a great deal during the summer. He was in town recuperating from an attack of tuberculosis which was not severe but which gave him the chance to rest after his recent emotional "crackup." We spent hours talking about his books and friends, his drinking and his hopes. He was curious about *Contempo* and the respect we had for Thomas Wolfe at Chapel Hill. But he objected to my working on the *Federal Theatre Magazine* because he thought that I would be doing publicity, which he feared might destroy whatever talent I had as a writer.

When the symphony cuts came, however, I telegraphed Hallie again to see whether she had any news for me. Despite all her problems, she wired me from Washington, saying that she had once more requested my services. She instructed me to wait until I had been cleared by WPA officials and said I would have to pay my fare to New York.

By now I was too restless to wait it out in Asheville. That the Federal Theatre was shaky did not matter to me; I promptly closed the bookshop deal, dropped the freelance writing, and shook Stringfield's hand. One February night I boarded the train that Wolfe described in *Of Time and the River*—the train which first took him north from his native mountain town. I had a hunch that if I did not leave now I would miss my chance to become a part of Uncle Sam's pioneering venture in a nationwide theatre.

2

THE headquarters of the New York City Federal Theatre project were a block west of Times Square. I reached it in a roundabout way, passing empty stores and dark theatres, their fronts plastered with "For Rent" signs, posters of new films, and faded three-sheets peeling off the houseboards. Theatres were playing such hits as *Tobacco Road* and *Dead End,* and burlesque thrived under the banner of the Minskys—the Shuberts of this seminude frolic. Though Mayor Fiorello LaGuardia kept a vice squad to crack down on strippers showing too much, burlesque was a Sunday spectacle compared to today's freedom of nudity on stage and screen.

Along 42nd Street—the Gay White Way of the Follies and the Scandals—once glamorous theatre palaces were now run-down grind houses showing double features of old westerns, horror films, and sexy thrillers, with glittering marquees and posters of flaming pistols and double-breasted sirens. Flanking the gaudy movie houses, smelling of unwashed bums who used them for sleeping, were souvenir and novelty shops, nickle hotdog, hamburger, and juice joints, catering to sharpies, people looking for jobs, professional beggars rattling tin cups, and visitors from the hinterlands looking for the fabled street of song and dance.

The four-story building on the northwest corner of 44th Street and Eighth Avenue turned out to have been a branch of the defunct Bank of United States. When in December 1930, it shut its doors, along with fifty-nine other branches, the Bank of United States was the largest bank in the nation to suspend payments. Many of its depositors were immigrants who had been under the impression that it was a government bank because of its name. Now the government

7

had leased the building to house units of the New York City Federal Theatre.

The street floor was still set up like a bank; it was noisy and crowded with an odd assortment of young and old people. Behind wickets, where tellers had once handled money, WPA clerks were handing out forms to lines of actors and others seeking jobs on the project. Some stood by high counters, baffled by the forms and asking the guard at the revolving doors for help. Among the faces, I remember those of militant, eager-eyed young actors who saw this as their big chance and uppish stage veterans who had seen their best days before the movies became talkies. Dressed in worn furs, hats, and coats of another era, the old actors stood apart, as if resentful of the young crowd and hid their need under a show of pride and past glory.

"Letting them use your name in the program?" asked a heavily made-up actress.

"No, I'm joining a group to protest it," replied a chubby character actor.

"Maybe you won't need to," said a frowning chap in a blue serge suit. "Those reds'll fix it."

"Yes, with propaganda," said the actress. "Uncle Sam better throw them out fast."

The guard pointed to the marble staircase at the rear and said that Mrs. Flanagan's office was on the mezzanine. I learned that Hallie was in Washington but that I might see Rosamond Gilder, head of the Bureau of Research and Publications. She was two short blocks down Eighth Avenue; the building was another bank. But this one was in business.

I rode up in the elevator and found a small, pleasant woman behind a desk piled high with books and scripts. Miss Gilder was another member of the National Theatre Council whom Flanagan had consulted when she was organizing the project. An assistant to Edith Isaacs, the editor of *Theatre Arts Monthly,* Miss Gilder was on leave to supervise research and publication for the project.

"You'll have to see Mrs. Flanagan," she said in a soft voice after I told her my story. She also explained that I might go to the WPA relief bureau down Sixth Avenue to check on my status and apply for work.

Crossing windy Seventh Avenue I noticed the sliding ribbon of lights spell out news flashes around the Times Building. Hitler was bent on extending the borders of the Fatherland, Mussolini's black-shirted legions were pushing deeper into Ethiopia to revive the glory of ancient Rome. England and France were playing the game of peace at any price with the pair, and F.D.R. was busy on the homefront patching up the embattled New Deal. Three million Americans were on WPA, twelve million still jobless.

I spotted a barricade where a WPA work crew with shovels and jackhammers was repairing a piece of Broadway. Reaching the hooded station of the Sixth Avenue Elevated, I boarded a downtown train. The avenue rumbled with the underground construction of the new city subway which

Home Relief

would replace the noisy and sprawling El from the West Side to Greenwich Village. My destination was the Siegel-Cooper Building on 18th Street. With its high arched entrance, roofed open gallery, and solid stone structure of the last century, it still stands on the avenue as an imposing city landmark.

The interior was a block-long cavern, cold and dismal, with tall cast-iron pillars set off by lightbulbs hanging from the high ceiling like fuzzy giant spiders. It was jammed with a crowd more motley and shabby than at the defunct bank —an unemployed mass from all over the map. They came with ragged children nibbling on crusts and with infants at their breasts, as if to give proof of their desperate need. Voices rang out in the deep stationlike cave, directed at WPA personnel who could do nothing about the red tape of being certified for relief.

I glanced over a set of forms and found that, in addition to biographical details, education and job history, I had to answer questions that amounted to taking a pauper's oath in order to qualify for relief. I had come for a job, not relief, I told a clerk. He replied that I could not get one without the other, adding that there was a two-year residence requirement to be eligible. I was referred to a supervisor to whom I showed Flanagan's telegram; the woman shook her head and handed it back to me.

I stumbled out of the old building wondering for the first time whether I had not made a mistake in coming to the big city. As I walked up the rumbling avenue, I remembered the face of a displaced American I saw that morning on Times Square—cold, hungry, far from home, and out of work.

3

"YES, Mrs. Flanagan's back. Do you have an appointment?" the receptionist asked when I returned the following morning to the mezzanine. I shook my head and gave her my name. A dozen persons were in the room, five huddled together in a heated discussion. No doubt they all had appointments; it would be a long wait.

Minutes later a door opened and Hallie Flanagan appeared, the image of a busy executive in a tailored suit and felt hat, the brim pressed down over her bobbed reddish hair. She was escorting an older man to whom she said goodbye and stepped toward me with a friendly nod. She led me into her office; it had a front-row balcony view of 44th Street, the scene of recent protests and demonstrations against censorship.

Hallie, a tiny woman—she was four feet eight inches tall —with the spirit of the great open spaces in her airy movements struck me as a bright Vassar girl rather than the boss of the world's largest theatre. Her small freckled face showed no sign of strain or defeat over the recent crises. She appeared to thrive on crises, and her air of confidence suddenly dispelled whatever misgivings I had about the future of the project. Sitting behind a desk piled high with scripts and sketches plus two telephones, Hallie said she was glad that I had come despite warning me to wait until my status had been cleared.

"I didn't think you'd play it safe—anymore than I would've," she said, as sure of herself as the curve of her forceful chin.

"I hope I haven't put you on the spot."

"We're all on the spot. From what I hear I haven't played it safe to okay some productions," she said, her kind brown

11

eyes meeting mine. "But we're not here to do only pap for babes and octogenarians—to quote Elmer Rice. I suppose you know we lost him."

"Yes." I sat opposite her. "Too bad."

"But we can't let that stop us." The telephone rang; she picked it up, nodded, then said, "Tell them it won't be five minutes—or they can go."

Hallie put down the phone with a slight note of irritation. She told me that another grievance committee was waiting to see her. She had already listened to four or five that morning. A veterans' group came to protest about Communists heading some units, and a radical group to warn her that the vets were giving the Hearst press scripts that were damaging to the project.

"The stagehands' union said it would throw a picket line around the Lafayette in Harlem if we let Negroes work backstage. A Yiddish vaudeville unit asked for autonomy from the Jewish Theatre," she said. "The saddest spectacle was a committee of old actors and vaudevillians who don't want their names in the programs. I told them if they were ashamed of the Federal Theatre they could go back on home relief. Now as for you. I'm sorry about the red tape. Also because I forgot you while on my rush tour of the Coast."

"I hated to bother you."

"I wish you had," she said in a tone that meant it. "I might've gotten you here sooner. I had to take somebody I knew nothing about and I'm saddled with him. He was recommended to me by John Nance Garner. Did you see those mimeographed things I sent you?"

I nodded.

"Don't tell me what you think," she said with more irritation in her voice than before. "This amateurish stuff must stop now that we have our own press. The next issue will be printed. I want you to help edit something that will look like a magazine. With lively articles, lots of photographs, and a cover that's as smart as *New Theatre* and your *Contempo.*"

"Have you told him?"

"Plenty."

Hallie Flanagan

"Think he'll listen to me?"

"Let's gang up on him," she said, her face relaxing into a half-smile. "I asked Rosamond Gilder to help me."

"I met her yesterday."

"I'm glad. A bright woman. Did you know her father edited *The Century?*"

"I didn't."

"I asked Rosamond to help get rid of Pierre de Rohan. But she insists I hired him and will have to do it myself. Now that you're here, maybe we can do something."

"I'll try."

"I hear the press is like a new toy. He's always in the press room. If he stays there, you might be able to turn out something decent with Mark Marvin, who's written for *New Theatre.*"

"I know Mark. He edited a literary review out West. We swapped advertising space."

"I thought you might know him. You two should get out a lively magazine. You can divide the field between you—one to look after New York and the other nationwide." She went on, as though her problem with de Rohan was settled. "Check all production groups from Harlem to Greenwich Village. There's a unit down at the Provincetown Playhouse where Madalyn O'Shea is teaching drama coaches and directors."

She dug out a folder from the material on her desk and went on: "We have a raft of dancers and choreographers. Do a piece on how the dance is coming back to the theatre. And on our bright young directors: Eddie Goodman, Jimmie Light, Vincent Sherman, Jack Houseman, and Orson Welles. Catch the circus! We don't have an elephant yet, but the kids don't miss it. Do a story on them with lots of pictures. They love the show. You'll love it too. Better than *Jumbo* at the Hippodrome."

"Where does the circus play?"

"Armories in winter and come spring under the big top in city parks for a dime. My secretary'll give you the schedule." She stopped to pick up the ringing telephone, nodded twice, and turned back to me as she hung up. "Now to getting you on the payroll. I'll have to request you as nonrelief supervisory or you'll never make it from out of state. You'll have to wait six or seven weeks for your first check. Can you manage?"

"I sold the bookshop."

"My secretary has the forms. Fill them out. We'll get them off today," she said. "We want no chummy house organ but a first-rate magazine. And keep your eyes and ears open. There are many, inside and outside the project, who want us to flop. Let's surprise them all. Most of all those stuffy Broadway producers and congressmen who think Uncle Sam should keep his nose out of show business."

The telephone rang twice as she handed me a folder of articles and clippings. She picked it up, listened, and turned to me, "It's Washington."

While she took the call I looked over the clippings. In one of them the producer, Brock Pemberton, was quoted as saying that the government's idea of spending money to produce plays with relief talent was "absurd." He said that there was no talent on relief rolls, no curtain would go up, and if it did, nobody would go to see a show put on by a troupe of "down-and-outers."

His opinion was shared by another prominent producer, John Golden. When Flanagan approached Golden to join the Federal Theatre Advisory Committee, he replied in a public letter to the *New York Times,* "It is my fear that most of those [productions] put on in New York, Chicago, Los Angeles, and other large cities may not conform to professional standards and so do more harm than good to the theatre as an institution."

There was a statement by Eva LeGallienne, the actress-producer of the classical Civic Repertory: "I am terrified by the large sums spent by the government to assist dramatic work in this country. . . . It is a vast mistake to feed people upon malnutritious and downright bad food when they can get the best." Perhaps Miss LeGallienne was miffed: Hopkins had ignored her plan to save the ailing theatre. When I recently wrote Miss LeGallienne, she had not changed her mind about the Federal Theatre—despite all of its achievements.

There were comments from others who did not regard the project as a lost cause. The drama critics, notably Brooks Atkinson of the *New York Times* and Burns Mantle of the *Daily News,* looked upon it as a new theatre venture, not as a relief project. Lee Shubert, a man who controlled most of the Broadway houses, saw it as a chance to rent some of his dark theatres as well as to help show business. He said that people seeing Federal Theatre shows would get to like the theatre and start going to other Broadway shows—even if they could afford only to "buy our cheap seats."

I set down the folder when Hallie hung up and said that the call was from Jacob Baker, the administrative deputy for Federal One. He was checking the status of *Jefferson Davis,* a play the New York City project was preparing for a tour to placate Southern Democrats after Elmer Rice had announced that the Living Newspaper was planning productions on such subjects as sharecroppers and the Scottsboro Case.

"The play's sponsored by the United Daughters of the Confederacy, and we're lucky to have the grand-niece of Jeff Davis's in the cast," Flanagan said with a knowing smile. "It ought to please everybody down there, but I hope no critic shows up next week at the Biltmore preview."

"Should I see it?"

"Go to the circus."

"Thanks, Hallie," I said, as I stood up. "I think another committee's out there waiting for you."

"The worst part of my job—because you know how I feel about labor and just grievances," she said and held out her small hand. "I hope you don't regret selling your bookshop for a job that may not outlast the year."

"No regrets," I said and shook her hand. "I hope you have none about Elmer Rice."

"I have. But I believe Philip Barber and Walter Hart will do a good job. I have a new national deputy, William Farnsworth, who was with the NRA Amusement Code Authority, to free me from Washington chores so I can spend more time here."

"Here's where you belong."

"And don't think we're lowering the flag because of that Living Newspaper censorship," she said as she showed me to the door. "Our next one will have plenty to say. There'll be impersonations of congressmen, the Nine Old Men of the Supreme Court, Thomas Jefferson, and Earl Browder. Let Washington try and stop it."

4

HALLIE Flanagan took the oath of office, swearing to defend the United States Constitution against all enemies, domestic and foreign, on August 27, 1935—her 45th birthday. Whether Hopkins had planned it, no one knows, but she makes a point in *Arena,* her personal history of the Federal Theatre, of the place where it was administered—in a theatre, the old Auditorium in Washington. At the time the cavernous building was being remodeled to accomodate hundreds of WPA and PWA workers as headquarters for Federal One. Shortly afterwards, the Arts projects moved to a Florentine-style palazzo which had belonged to Evelyn Walsh McLean, owner of the Hope diamond.

Flanagan came to her militant social outlook and her notion of a relevant theatre in a roundabout fashion. For Hallie was no child of a big city with slums and settlement houses, where social and industrial unrest along with cultural advantages, were close at hand. She was a small-town girl from the conservative Midwest near the turn of the century—a hinterland as American as a Rodgers and Hammerstein song from *Oklahoma!*

Hallie was born of Scotch-German ancestry in Redfield, South Dakota. Her family moved to a few Midwest states before she, like Hopkins, settled down in the college town of Grinnell, Iowa. She and Hopkins attended high school and college there, but not as classmates; he was a year ahead of her. To Hopkins she was "Hallie Ferguson, a pretty coed whose only plan was to marry Murray Flanagan, a handsome Irishman of the Grinnell Class of 1909."

With the spirit and energy of a responsible young woman, Hallie learned early to face life and adjust to the world around her. In March, 1918, her father had a disastrous financial loss. The following year her husband died of tuberculosis, leaving her with two small boys. She had no teaching degree, yet the head of the Grinnell College English Department let her teach a drama course because of her experience at the local high school.

While teaching in Grinnell her seven-year-old son died; she was left with Frederick, aged five. Hallie wrote a prize-winning play, *The Curtain,* which, along with her original work as a drama teacher, brought her to the attention of Professor George P. Baker of the 47 Workshop. Baker engaged her to assist him during his last year at Harvard before going to teach at Yale.

At the workshop Hallie wrote a satirical comedy, *Incense,* and then returned to Grinnell, where she established an Experimental Theatre. For her work there she received a Guggenheim grant—the first awarded to a woman—to make a comparative study of European theatres in 1926. The year's survey, covered in her first book, *Shifting Scenes,* taught her that "a truly creative theatre was one which responded socially and artistically to a changing world." That was to become the central idea behind her future theatre work.

Flanagan was impressed with the theatre of the young Soviet Union. It was passionate, concerned, and committed to probing social problems. Only later would it harden into Socialist realism and the approved propaganda which would sap and destroy the vitality which thrilled Hallie in 1926. The Moscow Art Theatre was world-famous, having already toured the United States a few years earlier, but it was in its more experimental groups where Hallie found the kind of active "people's theatre" that helped shape her impressions of theatre as a great national institution. Meyerhold, for example, a former Stanislavski pupil who rejected the realism of "facial expression" at the Moscow Art Theatre, was one of her favorites. With his emphasis on breaking down audience-actor barriers with acrobatics and clowning in an effort to reach workers and students, he provided a model for her later work, both at Vassar and in New York.

Upon her return Flanagan went to Poughkeepsie, where

19

she was engaged to direct the Vassar Experimental Theatre. She now started to produce plays of social significance. In collaboration with Mary Ellen Clifford, a Vassar graduate, she dramatized *Can You Hear Their Voices?*, based on a story by Whittaker Chambers from an actual incident in the 1930 drought. The story appeared in *The New Masses,* the left-wing magazine where Chambers was a staff member before going on to Henry Luce's *Time. Voices* was impassioned and controversial, an outgrowth of the Agit-Prop theatre she had seen in Germany and Russia.

What made *Voices* all the more newsworthy in 1931 was its appearance on the stage of a woman's college in upstate New York. Vassar was fashionable but also progressive; many of its young women had been engaged in the suffragette movement of the twenties. One of its militant graduates was Edna St. Vincent Millay. During the winter of 1935, a free verse poem of hers appeared in *Harper's* which declared, "If you don't believe in God, it is a good thing to believe in Communism." Also Henry Noble MacCracken, the Vassar President, who okayed the presentation of *Voices,* had been a professor of drama there and performed in some of its productions.

Jane Mathews, in her excellent study of *The Federal Theatre,* describes how *Voices* unfolded in seven fast-moving scenes showing the plight of dirt farmers who starved while the Hoover administration "dilly-dallied" over relief measures. A series of black and white vignettes, set off by blackouts, were interwoven with news of congressional apathy flashed on a white screen. At the close, the prison-bound father tells his sons to go to Communist headquarters in the hope that they might help make a better world. The Voice of the Loudspeaker rises at this point to say: "These boys are symbols of thousands of people who are turning somewhere for leaders. Will it be the educated minority? Can you hear their voices?"

With this controversial play Flanagan aimed to sound a warning that Americans were losing faith in a political system which did nothing to relieve their economic misery. Conservatives were shocked by the message; they found it revolutionary. Leftwingers, who expected the working classes to turn to them for guidance, found it misleading and not radical enough. The *New York Times* described *Voices* as "a play in which propaganda did not defeat drama, as usually happens, because it was all propaganda—scaring, biting, smashing propaganda."

Though propaganda was a nasty word those days in many circles, the reviewer saw in *Voices* the kind of vital theatre that was inspired by the growing despair of people caught up in the Depression. Flanagan knew that "propaganda" was a word usually applied to anything with ideas, social content, and controversial issues calling for action. She was no more afraid of the word than the prominent writers and intellectuals of the early thirties who saw the collapse of American capitalism and studied the Russian experiment as a possible solution to our social and economic ills.

By 1936, President Roosevelt's New Deal, despite constant sniping by conservatives and Southern Democrats in Congress, was able to put through the basic legislation for setting up the present welfare state. Much of this program was similar to demands made by left-wing groups that agitated during the Hoover years. WPA boss Hopkins was outspoken in defending the Federal relief programs: "Where can they [the unemployed] turn if they can't turn to their government? What's their government for?"

Committed as Flanagan was to New Deal philosophy, which hoped to end the "old inequities" and make for a better America, she had questions and concerns. She recalls them in *Arena:* "What part can art play in this program? Could we, through the power of the theatre, spotlight the tenements and thus help in the plan to build decent houses for all people? Could we, through actors and artists who had themselves known privation, carry music and plays [to grownups and their] children in the city parks? Were not happy people at work the greatest bulwark of democracy?"

While in Europe Hallie saw the theatre not as a luxury, patronized mainly by the leisure classes, but as an educational force, a necessity like public schools, libraries, parks, and museums. Hence Federal Theatre productions were to be open to all, either free or at a price people could afford—ten, twenty-five, and fifty cents, but not higher than a dollar. She saw this as a way to reach millions of Americans whose theatre fare was limited to movies. And by bringing live theatre to this vast untapped audience, Flanagan believed that she could help to reopen theatres everywhere.

WPA officials in Washington probably expected Flanagan to provide escapist entertainment to amuse the masses brought up on a movie diet. But in the middle of the Depression, and during the days when Hitler and Mussolini started their deadly games, it was, to quote Atkinson of the *New York Times,* "naïve to assume that any form of public expression would be innocuous. Particularly in the case of unemployed citizens; they could not be neutral about a world which had rejected them."

Though both Hopkins and President Roosevelt were confident that Flanagan could provide the kind of theatre they wanted for the times—sharing as she did their low opinion of congressmen whose ignorance and prejudices made them suspicious of learning and the arts—I doubt if they were prepared for the way she was to rock the ship of state to carry out their program. For Hallie was not only dedicated to the New Deal; she was an inspired theatre woman who had little patience with politicians and bureaucrats, and was more outspoken than the three men who headed the other projects.

Of the four projects comprising Federal One, the theatre was most often in the news. Like all things theatrical, it had an affinity for the limelight. But behind the scenes from coast to coast was the tiny figure of Hallie Flanagan—a major reason why Uncle Sam's adventure into a nationwide theatre made headlines in the thirties and still continues to do so with the rediscovery of its struggles and achievements.

5

I DID not try to see Pierre de Rohan until about noon the
following day. After having a snack at the crowded Automat
between two grind houses on 42nd Street, I headed for the
L-shaped bank building at the northwest corner of Eighth
Avenue. Though I was not yet officially on the project, I was
anxious to meet the man and start helping to produce a magazine to please Hallie.

I encountered only the receptionist in the large gloomy
room of battered desks, typewriters, and a tilted drawing
board by the window. She was a pleasant, heavy-set black
woman with glasses and a Philadelphia ring to her speech.
At first she said that de Rohan was in the press room and
then, glancing at the empty rack near a small inner office,
she told me he was out to lunch. I asked about Mark Marvin;
he was out in the field. I decided to wait. She handed me a
paper and I sat near an odd-shaped typewriter.

After glancing through the paper, I turned to copies of
theatre articles which Hallie had given me to take along
with her report of project activities, slated to appear in the
next issue of the magazine. The articles described the state
of the theatre: the boom of the twenties, the big bust of the
thirties, and mass unemployment in the entertainment industry. Part of the story was told in the box office prices: they
had risen to three dollars, musicals were higher, and popular
fifty-cent seats that young people could afford had vanished
along with the audience, which thought twice before spending a dollar to see a show during the Depression.

The price hike had occurred during the boom. Speculators,
cigar-smoking angels, and real-estate operators who knew
nothing about the theatre and cared less about it had taken
over Broadway. With their postwar profits they almost drove

the legitimate producer out of business and the diminishing audience out of the theatre. The worst quality of show business was rampant in their aim to outdo each other with "satin and lumber." They specialized in routine plays and extravagant musicals which had since found a more profitable audience in motion pictures at fifty cents.

The production boom reached its all-time high in the 1927–1928 Broadway season. That year 264 shows were produced, compared to the average hundred a year presented between 1900 and 1936. The ratio of flops during those years had been an average of four to one, and rose a notch higher during the boom. Of the seventy-five or eighty theatres active in the twenties, less than half were now being used in a season by legitimate attractions. Several had been converted to motion pictures or burlesque houses, radio rented a few as auxiliary studios, and the rest were dark and badly in need of repairs. A few had been leased by the Federal Theatre and were being put back into shape while shows were in rehearsal.

The human element fared worse. Actors Equity estimated that 8,000 actors were out of work, but twice that number was more likely—not counting the estimated 30,000 vaudevillians, stage technicians, and musicians affected by motion pictures. First to go in this technological shakeup were the variety circuits bringing three-a-day to towns and cities. Then the road, once flourishing with as many as eighteen companies of a musical, was now reduced to one or two inferior duplicates that often got a cool reception. Finally went the resident stock companies, leaving only motion pictures to entertain the country. Thousands of actors flocked to Hollywood; many found themselves stranded and grateful for a day's work as a Cecil B. deMille extra.

A tall, attractive brunette was the first to return from lunch; she went to the drawing board and lit a cigarette. Then came a shy, blondish chap who sat before the odd machine. He told me it was a varityper, a machine used for preparing copy in various sizes and styles of type. He used a special paper; each line was a strip of tissue loosely gummed down so that it would be lifted up and the letters stretched to a uniform margin at the right. The page was then photographed on a paper-thin zinc sheet for printing on the offset press.

I noticed he was setting up Flanagan's report for the upcoming issue. Turning to the copy which she had given me, I learned that, as of February 1936, 10,700 theatre workers—actors, singers, dancers, clowns, directors, choreographers, designers, technicians, readers and researchers, typists, clerks, timekeepers, box office and maintenance personnel—were now on the nationwide payroll of the project.

Of the $4,800,000,000 Congress had voted for the Emergency Relief Act in April 1935, about five percent—$27,000,000—was for the four Arts projects; the rest was for WPA blue-collar workers on construction and other jobs. The Federal Theatre's share of the sum was $6,784,036, half of which was for the 5,000 employed in New York City, the center of theatre activities, and this was slated to last until June 30, when the current appropriation ended.

As the largest center in the thirty-one states to have theatre people, New York City had engaged more than 4,000 in forty-nine producing groups. California, the next largest, with 1,680 on the payroll, had thirty-two producing units; Boston, thirty-three; Chicago, fourteen; Seattle, five; Cleveland, four; Philadelphia, three; St. Louis and Dallas, two. Five or more projects were in Connecticut, Florida, New York, and New Jersey. Between Colorado and the West Coast there was no project in ten of the states; a recent survey had shown no theatre unemployment in those areas.

By now Flanagan had come to terms with the twelve major unions representing the theatre and worked out a security wage based on current prevailing scales. Among the unions were those covering all actors and performers from stage, vaudeville, and circus. Other unions represented dramatists, musicians, scenic artists, technicians, teamsters, wardrobe mistresses, managers, and treasurers. She did not agree to a closed shop, saying that Federal Theatre was not Broadway but a nationwide relief project with the task of employing theatre workers on the basis of need and excellence, whether or not they belonged to unions.

I glanced up from the report, my head reeling with figures,

when I heard the chap say, "Mark," and saw a husky, sandy-haired fellow with glasses joining him at the machine. I introduced myself to Mark; we sat down and reminisced about the days we both edited little magazines. Then I told him I had just come up from North Carolina and Hallie was requesting me for the magazine. He had come East to help his brother Herbert Kline, editor of *New Theatre*. As the magazine was having a difficult time, despite the Sunday Night League Benefits all over town, he was glad Flanagan had taken him on the project.

"Hallie wants us to work together," I said in a low voice. "To help get out a decent magazine."

"That's why she hired me," Mark said. "I haven't done much yet."

"What sort of bird is this Pierre de Rohan?"

"He can write well when he wants to—usually with a nasty streak—maybe because he worked on a Hearst sheet. But he's no editor."

Mark took me over to meet George Griggs at the varityper, Jessie Smith with the Philadelphia sound, and the chain-smoking Alice Fried at the drawing board. He told them Mrs. Flanagan had sent me to work on the magazine. He then showed me what he had done so far—the cover she was pasting up with black letters, FEDERAL THEATRE, a big square under the first letters and a wide bar down the right.

Pierre de Rohan walked in, wearing a dark homburg, a velvet collared coat, spats, and flashing a Malacca cane like a boulevardier. Mark led me to him and repeated what he had said to the others. I cannot remember de Rohan taking my outstretched hand, but I have a vivid recollection of the ends of his shapely moustache pointing downward as his eyes narrowed and he mumbled to himself: "Mrs. Flanagan didn't ask me," he said, raising his voice. "I'll tell her I can't use you. I'm very sorry."

He left me standing there with Mark, went into his office, and told Jessie to get Mrs. Flanagan's office on the telephone.

"Come have a beer," Mark said cheerfully. "There's a hangout down the block. You can eat and drink on credit. It's run by a couple of fine micks—Kiernan and Dineen."

6

WE sat at a back corner of the friendly bar. Most of the gang appeared to be newspapermen rather than actors, but there was a sprinkling of office workers. They were fairly well dressed; talked, joked, and laughed like old comrades whose joviality had an air of self-confidence. If Mark had not told me that the bar was a hangout for project people from the two bank buildings, I could not have guessed they were the "down-and-outers" Brock Pemberton said would never open a show. Work relief had done wonders for them: a few months earlier they were hunting for jobs with holes in their shoes and waiting for the weekly dole.

"De Rohan tried the same crap with me. And for the same reason. Hallie sent me," Mark said as we sipped our beers. "He wants a one-man magazine. I know she's on his tail."

Mark pointed out Mayer Portner as he walked in with a tall Negro and went to the bar. Portner was the other writer on the staff—a slight, bald man in his thirties with a snappish mouth and a pointed face. Mark said that Portner was being consumed by bitterness. The literary world was anathema to him. He hated successful writers, had contempt for failures, and delighted in attacking O'Neill, Caldwell, Dos Passos, Fitzgerald, Wolfe, and Hemingway. Sometimes he had a kind word for the dead—Flaubert, Chekhov, Marlowe.

Portner had come to Greenwich Village from Cornell; he had stoked the furnace there to pay his way until the Depression forced him to drop out. In the city he did stints as a freelance writer and press agent. Like many artists and writers of those bohemian days, he lived in Strunskyville—the block of run-down houses which then faced Washington Square and the old Provincetown Playhouse on Macdougal Street. Portner found an ardent admirer in a member of the art-loving Strunsky family, who allowed struggling talent to live there rent free. He showed his gratitude by dedicating a novel, *Not to the Swift,* to his patron.

"He's so anti-anti he sometimes spends the weekend talking to himself. His pet hate is radicals of all shades. But he hates Liberty Leaguers and Veteran Leaguers too. He says they're all slobs trying to wreck the project by putting his darling Hallie in the middle."

"You mean he likes Hallie?"

"He met her once and is nuts about her."

"And Pierre de Rohan?"

"He's sure Pierre changed his name from Peter Rosenberg to that of the French cardinal. But who cares?"

"Set me straight, Marvin," I said, after a silence. "Are radicals out to kill the project?"

"That depends on your politics."

"Of course. But about how many on it—reds, pinks, fellow travelers?"

"Nobody can be sure about how many Democrats or Republicans are on it."

Mark went on to explain that the Emergency Relief Act (ERA) forbade inquiry into a client's political affiliation. This was put into the law at the request of Republican congressmen who feared that the Democrats, being in power, might deny equal benefits to their jobless members. Now it was the Republicans who were making a big issue that radicals were on the project and organizing into small new unions which were militant in their demands.

While WPA labor policy maintained an open shop, it recognized workers' rights to organize and petition through unions. The majority of professionals on the Federal Theatre were members of craft unions or allied associations. But many others had no such affiliation—some Jewish and Negro actors, professional dancers, and young actors working in summer stock and small off-Broadway groups. They promptly joined the new unions along with the other unorganized workers—typists, clerks, guards, administrative, and maintenance staffs.

Early in 1935 the Workers' Alliance was formed to organize the unemployed relief clients on WPA and PWA. Later that year an affiliate was formed, the City Projects Council, a union for unorganized white-collar workers on Federal One. About the same time the Supervisors' Council was set up to represent unit and departmental heads on the same projects. These new unions were more aggressive in presenting members' grievances than the older unions, which still regarded the Federal Theatre as a charitable project rather than a theatrical enterprise.

The conservative policy of these craft unions gave impetus to the new ones, which not only took up grievances but the task of getting workers assigned, improving standards, and helping to develop a wider audience for project shows. Yet they worked closely with the American Federation of Labor (AFL) and the new Congress for Industrial Organization (CIO) and are credited with having helped to create a growing union consciousness among their members, many of whom were later to join the two big unions. Flanagan was aware that most union representatives, signers of petitions, pickets, and marchers were young people with "a burning core of indignation against social wrongs. Our actors were themselves protagonists in a drama more stirring than any which ever reached our stage," she wrote in *Arena*.

Mark explained that the conservative members of Actors Equity and other craft unions at the time were lined up against the young actors, directors, technical crews, and clerical staffs. The older theatre people charged that the young ones were amateurs, inexperienced in the theatre, and had no right to be on the project. They also complained about the young office workers for taking jobs which should have been given to their members—not realizing that a government bureaucracy needed a trained clerical force.

With the rise of the small militant unions, the conflict that had originally started on professional grounds now turned into a political battle. They called each other names—Communist troublemakers, reactionary bastards—and made charges and countercharges of wrecking the project and being disloyal to the American system. To help counteract the activities of the young radicals, the old conservatives were joined by veterans' groups and supported by the Liberty League, recently formed by big business to war on President Roosevelt and the New Deal legislation. Liberty League and patriotic-sounding propaganda was always welcomed by the national press.

"A couple years ago, when artists, writers, and theatre people agitated for a city, state, or Federal project to give them jobs," Mark said, "it was the radicals who got up petitions, marched to City Hall, were clobbered by cops, and made the administration see that something had to be done before there was a revolution.

"At that time Equity members, stagehands, and the other IATSE craft-union boys were cadging meals and playing pingpong and pinochle at the Actors' Dinner Club. They were too proud and respectable to show their faces in such protests. In fact they were against workers' demonstrations as being radical and beneath the dignity of their professions. But the minute the projects were set up, they demanded that only members of their stuffy unions be given jobs. Some are the old farts that don't want their names in the programs."

"Well," said Mayer Portner as he stopped by our table. "Take everything Red says with a swig of vodka. The red's for his politics, not his curly hair."

Mark smiled, introduced us, and invited him to join us. Portner sized me up, taking his time to sit down. Mark told him about me, Hallie, and de Rohan's reaction.

"You," Portner said, showing stubby yellow teeth, "must be another red—or a spy."

"He's a southern cracker," Mark laughed, "and a friend of Hallie's just the same."

"That accounts for the Cardinal's brushoff," Portner said and turned back to Mark. "Didn't he work you over when you came on?"

"Yeah," he nodded, "and for the same reason."

Portner shook his head and said, "Naw. He took you for a Flanagan spy. Don't laugh, Mark. Spying's the latest paranoia on the project. Borrowed from your Bolsheviks. Hallie just cracked a ring that's been reading her mail for our WPA colonel at the Armory."

"Colonel Somervell?" Mark said.

"Shits in high places are ransacking that theatre book Hallie wrote a few years ago to see if she's a No. 1 Stalin agent," Portner said, lowering his voice. "They're being egged on by Hollywood and Broadway ghouls to get rid of her before the project takes a few customers from their lousy shows."

7

I NEVER learned what Hallie told de Rohan, but the next day he sent Mark to find me. There was no telephone yet in the small apartment I had moved into on West 46th Street, a half block from Times Square. It was a few doors from the *Variety* office and a short distance from the two bank buildings. Before reporting to de Rohan I called Hallie. She was out of town; I left a message to thank her and to say that I was on the job with Mark.

When I saw de Rohan again, he was charming but ill at ease. He took me to the press room; his eyes shone as he spoke about the multilith press and showed me the zinc plates for the color pages that were going into the magazine. He was at home in that stuffy room smelling of printer's ink and cigar smoke. But when we were back in the office, he turned stand-offish and made it clear that I was there, not as an associate, but as his guest. He never changed this attitude.

I could have done nothing and he would have liked it. He never gave me an assignment; I followed through on Hallie's suggestions and saw that my stories got into print. He some-times discussed plans with Mark and me, but left us mostly on our own. Mark and I told him what articles we were doing and he would leave space for them. Despite this arrange-ment, we managed to help produce a passable theatre maga-zine.

Before settling down to write the stories, I rounded out my theatre background by reading articles Hallie had written for the *Times, New Theatre,* and *Theatre Arts Monthly* about Federal Theatre plans, its aims, and policy. Its policy was based on three major points: that jobless theatre people wanted to work and millions of Americans would enjoy their efforts; that the workers were to be regarded, not as reliefers, but as professionals capable of carrying out the program; that a theatre sponsored by Uncle Sam should not present trite or vulgar plays, but the kind that "the government could stand behind in a planned theatre program national in scope, regional in emphasis, and democratic in allowing each local unit freedom under these general principles."

These aims and the economic origins of the project, plus the size and variety of America, set the Federal Theatre apart as unique compared to the European state-supported theatres. It had only one thing in common with them: government subsidy. In France and Germany the top artists were chosen as members of government theatres. In Russia state officials told directors what plays to do. These were all national theatres in the tradition of a group of artists chosen to represent the state. The Federal Theatre, growing out of a people's need over the vast American continent, could function only as a democratic theatre.

The operation of the project was somewhat like that of the Federal government, with its policy and program planned in Washington and its execution varying with local and state conditions. The map was divided into five regions, with producing centers in New York, Los Angeles, Chicago, Boston, and New Orleans. All projects followed a chain of command from unit to state directors, and from state to regional directors, who were responsible to Flanagan as national head. She, in turn, reported to the Federal One administrator of the WPA. A similar chain of command operated within the WPA. Some officials were found to be unsympathetic to the Arts project, particularly the Federal Theatre, which they sabotaged in their area.

I next checked the New York City project, which Flanagan had set up with Elmer Rice. There were five major production units: the Living Newspaper, supervised by Morris Watson; the Popular Price Theatre, under Edward Goodman, to feature plays by new American authors; the Experimental Theatre, headed by Virgil Geddes and James Light, to offer *avant-garde* plays; the Negro Theatre, under John Houseman and Rose McClendon, to present Negro plays in Harlem;

and the Try-Out Theatre, sponsored by the League of New York Theatres, to try out scripts for commercial producers.

There were also a few units inherited from the CWA and FERA which had been started as direct relief to give free shows. About five hundred actors had been given employment in these programs, playing spot bookings in schools, hospitals, settlement houses, and other community centers. Most popular was the Gilbert and Sullivan company; others were the vaudeville and variety units, marionettes and minstrel shows, and a circus that thrilled thousands of adults and children of the five boroughs.

Virgil Geddes, Hallie Flanagan, and Harry Hopkins

Act One

Flanagan had named Eddie Dowling, the actor-producer, as national head of the circus and vaudeville; he was unwilling to cope with red tape and was the first to quit. She replaced him with Frank Merlin, a showman of wide experience, and proceeded to set up new companies to use part of the variety personnel: one-act experimental theatre, classical repertory, a children's theatre, a Negro Youth theatre, a poetic theatre, a German company doing classics in German, a Yiddish vaudeville unit, and an Anglo-Jewish Theatre.

While these units were taking shape, Flanagan and Rice dickered with the Shuberts for New York theatres. Broadway producers were reluctant to have project competition in the Times Square area. At first they did not want Federal Theatre to have a house between 40th and 50th Streets; they relented and allowed it to use the Biltmore on West 47th Street near Eighth Avenue for the Living Newspaper. The other theatres were the Manhattan, 53rd and Broadway, for the Popular Price; Daly's, 67th near Central Park, for the Experimental; and there was no problem about the Lafayette in Harlem, or the Willis in the Bronx and the Shubert-Teller in Brooklyn, for the Try-Out Theatre.

Though the Living Newspaper got Flanagan into trouble with WPA officials and congressmen, it was the answer to two major problems: putting hordes of actors to work and eliminating expensive scenery. This experimental documentary form, using actors, music, movement, light, and other multimedia effects is what persuaded Rice to take the post as New York City boss. He promptly contacted Heywood Broun, national president of the newly formed American Newspaper Guild, and got the New York City chapter to sponsor the productions. Morris Watson, national vice president of the Guild, was named head of the project. Watson was in the news at the time; he was an Associated Press editor who had been fired for alleged union activities and his case was being reviewed by the Supreme Court. (Though Watson won his case, he preferred to stay on as head of the unit rather than return to his AP post.)

The Living Newspaper staff, composed mostly of jobless newsmen, was set up like a city daily, with editor-in-chief,

35

managing editor, city editor, reporters, researchers, and copyreaders. It also had playwrights whose job, as Atkinson wrote in the *New York Times,* was to "shake the living daylights out of books, reports, newspapers and magazine articles" to gather material for the dramatic treatment, both historic and contemporary, of timely national and world events.

The time element necessitated the selection of topics with controversial and continuing interest. *Ethiopia* had been chosen because it was a newsworthy subject and its stormy history illustrated many of the difficulties Hallie faced. The idea took shape with the sudden appearance of a troupe of African drummers and musicians who had been stranded here. Despite a two-year residence clause, the relief bureau sent them to work on the New York City project.

A few of them could speak English; the others mumbled a sing-song patois, as though it were part of their act. Nevertheless, heated discussions followed as to their use in the production. Flanagan and Watson decided to have them beat drums, chant and shout in Haile Selassie's courtyard. This was to be done with no hint of caricature; the speeches and chants were to be as simple and literal as those sung in the Gertrude Stein-Virgil Thomson opera *Four Saints in Three Acts,* which John Houseman directed and which had a vogue on Broadway a bit earlier.

When the possibility of censorship arose over the issue of *Ethiopia*'s antagonizing Mussolini, Flanagan appealed to Eleanor Roosevelt and had her read the script. The First Lady interceded; Steve Early, a White House press officer, said it could go on provided that no foreign statesmen were represented in person. Flanagan considered it a reasonable request, Rice did not. He was fed up with months of bureaucracy, grievance committees and unreasonable union demands. As he said later in *Minority Report,* "Throughout my tenure of office, I was harassed by complaints and accusations . . . I incurred the wrath of the Civilian Conservation Corps . . . I was charged with discrimination . . . (but) A censorship situation led to my withdrawal from the project."

Convinced as he was that Washington would never allow

him to raise a curtain on a play of timely significance, Rice resigned and announced a private showing of *Ethiopia* for critics, reporters, and Federal Theatre people. He used the occasion to tell the press that "I don't think the decision to ban *Ethiopia* was made until after Morris Watson and I outlined some of the Living Newspaper's future productions to Washington officials. Plays dealing with the Scottsboro Case, sharecroppers, unemployment, and relief problems." Rice was convinced that the censorship sprung from very real fears of alienating the Southern Democrats as well as Mussolini.

The press reacted violently to Rice's remarks but he stuck by his guns and defended the "idea of Federal Theatre" as opposed to the politicalization of its operation. "It was constantly attacked in Congress as wasteful, immoral and Communistic . . . Had funds been provided for continuance, upon an artistic basis divorced from unemployment relief, the foundation would have been laid for a nationwide theatrical structure that would have brought enlightment and enjoyment to millions."

Flanagan defended the project, however, and tried to rally her directors. She was certain that controversy was inherent in her quest for a people's theatre and that individual episodes should not be allowed to become precedents for future work. Dramatic resignations, she hoped, might call attention to the potential for censorship in the project, but they did not help to further the very real job that needed to be done.

Despite Hallie's encouraging words, the *Ethiopia* incident, coming as it did before the curtain had gone up on a single major production, gave many reason to worry about the future. Mark and I knew that her most difficult task was not to create a theatre, but to cope with her detractors within the project and the political administration. How long she could manage it prompted Mark to ask me early that spring—as Hallie had asked me before—whether I regretted selling my Asheville bookshop to gamble on such a venture. We agreed that this early confrontation with "the enemy" put Hallie on her guard and that it doubled her determination to carry out a program for a relevant people's theatre in America.

ACT TWO

Curtain Rising
March 1936

8

MARCH 1936 was a month of hits.

The New York City Federal Theatre could now boast of having raised the curtain on three successful new productions, more than any other producer had unveiled within a period of fifteen days. The plays won critical approval and did much to counteract the charges of "boondoogle" bandied about by the press, politicians, and unsympathetic bystanders. Though one of the shows also brought the cry of "propaganda," some older actors got over the stigma of breadlines and home relief and were now proud to have their names used in the programs.

Chalk Dust, a play attacking bureaucracy, dullness, and intolerance in a high school, by Harold Clarke and Maxwell Nurnburg, opening at Daly's March 4, was the first success. Next came *Triple-A Plowed Under,* a Living Newspaper on the American farmer and the New Deal's effort to better his lot, March 14 at the Biltmore; and then the Broadway premiere of T. S. Eliot's *Murder in the Cathedral,* a poetic tragedy based on the martyrdom of Archbishop Thomas à Becket of Canterbury, March 20 at the Manhattan.

At all the openings I saw Flanagan. She never missed them, flying from Washington or wherever she had been checking the project. Like a Broadway producer she took notes during the performances, discussed them with authors, directors, and the cast late into the night; and sometimes she waited up with us for the first reviews. Hallie was a busy woman those days, commuting to Poughkeepsie, where she taught a Vassar class, and spending the weekends with her new husband Professor Philip Davis, his three teenage children, and her son Frederick, then attending Brown University.

41

Uncle Sam Presents

Reviewing *Chalk Dust* in the *World-Telegram,* Robert Garland said that it saved the critics from having to be "lenient with Federal Theatre productions on the basis that 'they're doing pretty well considering everything.' No apologies are needed for *Chalk Dust.* It has done for the theatre what the authors would do for the schools: fit them to the times." The play had a large following; among its sponsors was John Dewey, who headed a committee of prominent educators in favor of the production.

In the cast were two talented young actresses, Amelia Romano and Eleanor Scherr, who went from that show to Broadway and back, gaining Equity membership along the way. It was the first production designed by Howard Bay, who did several others for the project and became one of Broadway's busiest designers. His settings for *Chalk Dust* expressed the lifeless atmosphere of the environment. The most striking set was a flat expanse of blackboard, divided into blank squares that seemed to emphasize a feeling of useless learning. *Chalk Dust* played in ten other cities and was later sold to Hollywood.

Flanagan was right when she said that the next Living Newspaper, *Triple-A Plowed Under,* was daring and controversial. We all knew the facts were explosive even when a play based on them was well documented and handled with wisdom and restraint. During rehearsals some older actors in the cast complained that there was no plot, no story line, and no character development. They asked, "Who in New York City cares about the farmer, about wheat, about the price of milk and bread?"

The creators of the script, along with Flanagan and the young director Joe Losey, realized that a new theatre form was making its debut on Broadway. Since the project's aim was to supplement rather than compete with the commercial theatre, Flanagan found it necessary to try out new production techniques for the Federal Theatre to succeed. The actors were told that two elements, light and music, were missing during the *Triple-A* rehearsals; once these were added everyone would agree it was good theatre.

Act Two

Scene from *Triple-A Plowed Under*

Soon afterwards we learned the real reason for their objections to *Triple-A.* The Federal Theatre Veterans' League, set up as a watchdog group to combat radicals on the project, considered it "unpatriotic." They spoke of shutting down the show and having the cast whisked off by the police. Two documented speeches in the script disturbed them. One was that of Henry Wallace, then Secretary of Agriculture and later Vice President, who called the Supreme Court's decision killing the New Deal's AAA to help the nation's farmers "the greatest steal in American history." The other speech was that of Earl Browder, secretary of the American Communist Party, in which he supported Congress against the Supreme Court on the same issue. One actor who rehearsed Browder's words asked to be excused from repeating them.

Uncle Sam Presents

When the curtain rose at the Biltmore, the *Times* stated that "the actors were full of misgivings, the audience full of tension, and the lobby full of police." Jane Mathews reports that despite some interruptions and occasional dragging out of troublemaking Vets, *Triple-A* opened with men marching against a glare of red lights to the sound of trumpets and voices urging the farmers to save the world by growing more wheat. Then followed a graphic review of farm events from the twenties to the thirties: mortgages foreclosed, farms auctioned, crops destroyed, devastation by drought, rise of farm cooperatives, creation of AAA, the Supreme Court declaring it unconstitutional, chants for jobs and not charity, farmers and workers joining to combat speculation and excess profits by middlemen and processors.

The production unfolded in a rapid succession of short scenes—pantomime, skits, blackouts, radio broadcasts, all cued to movement, light, and sound in a rhythmic pattern that electrified the audience and made it one with the performers. It was direct and effective propaganda for the farmer who sold his milk to processors for three cents a quart and the consumer (the audience) who paid many times more for it.

Triple-A was seen by a new theatre audience, many of whom had never before attended a live show and others who were young and class-conscious, having been nurtured on such social dramas as *Peace on Earth, Stevedore,* and *Waiting for Lefty.* It was the new audience that Harold Clurman described in his memoir *The Fervent Years*—young, eager, full of idealistic fervor, "with a smouldering conviction uncharacteristic of the usual Broadway audiences. . . . It was potentially the audience for a national theatre."

Commenting on the same audience, Richard Lockridge, critic of the *Sun,* said: "It is an enjoyable audience. It is young, lively, and I suspect hard up." Burns Mantle wrote in the *Daily News:* "The WPA has turned the theatre back to the people to whom it rightly belongs and taken it from the moneyed aristocracy that has for years dictated its course and definitely influenced its productions. For years playwrights have been told by commercial producers what the public didn't want and did—with no appeal from the decision. Uncle Sam, approaching a new public without commercial motives, established a whole set of new ideas of what constitutes popular theatre."

Though the critics praised the Living Newspaper form as a contribution to the modern theatre, the press in general attacked *Triple-A* as New Deal propaganda. The Hearst press, denounced U.S. dollars being spent for "pink plays," and blasted *Triple-A* as "the most outrageous misuse of taxpayers' money that the Roosevelt administration had been guilty of." The *Herald Tribune* echoed the Veterans League charges that the project was "run by reds."

Robert L. Bacon, Republican representative from Long Island, attacked *Triple-A* for its politics and said that the Roosevelt administration was "carrying its open warfare against the Supreme Court to the WPA stage." Bacon charged that the "subsidized political drama represented the New Deal," which he described as "the flower of American Brain Trust Communism."

Jacob Baker, Federal One administrator in Washington, asked his assistant Bruce McClure to investigate the cause of the furor. McClure reported finding no Communists in the plot, but learned from Flanagan and Victor Ridder, the New York City administrator, that WPA investigators had discovered that project friends of Veterans and Liberty Leaguers were selling scripts to the Hearst press, some of which were early drafts of plays and were not used in production.

McClure also learned that Hazel Huffman, a woman who worked in the project mail department, was reported to have gotten a large sum for an affidavit claiming that she had opened and read Flanagan's mail for three months and found it to be "revolutionary." Flanagan, anxious to keep project enemies from making more of it, decided to ignore the affair and to keep an eye on malcontents and troublemakers. McClure saw *Triple-A;* at the final curtain he joined the audience in the applause that lasted eight minutes.

While this controversy was raging, T. S. Eliot's *Murder in*

Exeunt Signing
(Backstage at *Murder in the Cathedral*)

the Cathedral quietly opened six blocks up Broadway at the Manhattan. It was staged by Halsted Welles as a kind of religious ritual with Harry Irvine, a Shakespearean actor, in the role of the Archbishop. The critics all agreed that Eliot had written a powerful drama that was distinguished by its poetic quality. John Mason Brown hailed it as one of the most notable productions of the season. Atkinson wrote in the *Times:* "Mr. Welles had conjured out of the choral chants and the violent imagery a moving and triumphant performance."

Everyone loved it but the left-wing press, which lamented that Federal Theatre had conceded to right-wing pressure and tastes. Theatregoers stormed the box office. The rush was due to critical acclaim and word-of-mouth enthusiasm, not advertising. The commercial theatre had forbidden the project to use more than an "abc" listing on the drama pages—and only on Mondays, the worst show day of the week.

It was our first offering to appeal to the carriage trade; limousines drove up with perfumed ladies in furs and jewels who swept into the lobby as though they were attending a Lynn Fontanne-Alfred Lunt premiere at the Theatre Guild. Eleanor Roosevelt saw the play, praised it, and went backstage to congratulate the cast.

Murder in the Cathedral was fortunate in having both a fine stylized production and the classic interior of the Manhattan Theatre, which was formerly the Hammerstein Theatre. The gothic-like design, with its high arches framing the wide proscenium, created the impression that the play was taking place in an actual cathedral. This was, I believe, Flanagan's idea; and it was taken up later by a community production given in a church. The Manhattan's acoustics were perfect for the sonorous speaking voices and the choral chants from the bold and original score by Lehman Engel, who also conducted the large orchestra.

It could have played the entire season, but the London agent had given it to the project for a limited engagement—despite rejection by the Theatre Guild and other Broadway producers. This added to the clamor for tickets, making it the hottest show in town. Scalpers moved in, queuing up to buy fifty-cent and dollar tickets, then peddling them for three to five dollars. The Federal Theatre had arrived on Broadway.

9

I SPENT most of the week doing what Flanagan had suggested—checking production units of the New York City project—and at the same time I got a bird's eye view of national activities from reports that reached our office. I checked shows in different stages of production: on drawing boards, at WPA scenic and costume shops, and in early and final rehearsals. I attended performances in theatres, halls, auditoriums, settlement houses, hospitals, orphanages, and community centers, sponsored by Rotary, the American Legion, the Police Department, and other civic and religious organizations.

Riding subways throughout the five boroughs I saw shows most New Yorkers did not know were being presented by the project: Shakespeare, Molière, Goldoni, Goldsmith, modern stock plays, Gilbert and Sullivan, musicals and marionettes, variety and vaudeville, and plays in foreign languages. I went to the circus—Hallie's favorite show—in a Brooklyn armory with thousands of kids giggling and screaming at the antics of the forty clowns.

In Harlem I had a double treat: a performance of *Conjur' Man Dies* at the Lafayette and a rehearsal of the voodoo *Macbeth* at the Elks Club. *Conjur' Man* was a farce directed by Joe Losey of *Triple-A*. It was straight entertainment, with Dooley Wilson playing a detective and singing, "I'll Be Glad When You're Dead, You Rascal You," a song that was popular at the time. (Later Wilson starred with Ethel Waters in *Cabin in the Sky* on Broadway; in the early forties he was Sam, who sang and played the piano in *Casablanca*.)

There was a supernatural atmosphere at the Elks Club where *Macbeth* was rehearsing under Orson Welles, who was also doing the "Shadow" and *March of Time* personalities live on radio. For *Macbeth* he and John Houseman had shifted the scene from Scotland to a Haitian jungle; the witches worked with a voodoo combo of drummers from the African troupe that did not get to perform in Haile Selassie's courtyard in *Ethiopia.* The pair assembled a notable cast: Jack Carter, Crown in the original *Porgy,* as the Thane; Edna Thomas, his ambitious wife, Maurice Ellis as Macduff, and Canada Lee as Banquo.

The Children's Theatre, supervised by Abel Plenn, was offering *Cinderella* and *Mark Twain,* based on the humorist's best-loved characters. The cast was dressed in creations by Irene Sharaff. Another company was rehearsing *The Emperor's New Clothes,* in a new version by Charlotte Chorpenning. Also for children was the Marionette Theatre, headed by Remo Bufano, the puppeteer, who had a production of *Treasure Island* running since 1935 on the CWA program. He was also making puppets and costumes for an original show, *Stars on Strings,* to open in May.

While there were French, Spanish, and Italian units in other cities, New York had German, Jewish, and Yiddish companies. Under the direction of John D. Bonn, the German Theatre was playing Heinrich von Kleist's *The Broken Jug* and rehearsing Rudolph Wittenberg's *Die Apostel.* The Anglo-Jewish unit was performing *The Eternal Wanderer* at the Jewish Center on Houston Street; the Yiddish group presented *The Idle Inn* on the subway circuit while preparing *We Live and Laugh,* a Yiddish musical revue to open at the Public Theatre on Second Avenue—once the Jewish theatre capital of the city.

The Gilbert and Sullivan company, directed by Edwin T. Emery, toured the boroughs as the most popular adult unit inherited from FERA and CWA. Its first production was *The Mikado* in October 1934, followed by *Pirates of Penzance* and *Pinafore* in 1935. The repertory was now being expanded to include *Iolanthe, Patience*, and *Trial by Jury.* Performances were so well received that the *American Gilbert and Sullivan Quarterly* said that the group was more lively and entertaining than the D'Oyly Carte from London.

Uncle Sam Presents

Shortly after Edward Goodman was praised for his production of *Murder in the Cathedral,* he was attacked by right-wing supporters on and off the project for putting into rehearsal a play about unemployment—the reason for the Federal Theatre's existence. The play was *Class of '29,* by Orrie Lashin and Milo Hastings, which concerned a group of jobless college graduates. I heard a reading of the script and saw no reason for the attack, unless its critics claimed that we on Uncle Sam's payroll should not try and bite the hand that fed us.

The Poetic Theatre, supervised by the poet-playwright Alfred Kreymborg, was rehearsing *The Dance of Death* by W. H. Auden, the young British poet whose work had been recommended by Eliot to Flanagan when she staged his *Sweeney Agonistes* at Vassar. I attended a session; the pianist ran over the Claire Leonard original score, actors spoke lines and moved on stage in a choreographed pattern. It baffled me, but, as we were all in an experimental mood, I eagerly awaited its May premiere.

Bringing the dance back to the theatre was one of the ideas Hallie had given me for a story. I rode all over Manhattan interviewing project choreographers. Charles Weidman spoke of his plans for *Candide* which was set to the music of Wallingford Riegger. Felicia Sorel was creating a dance production to Albert Roussel's *Suite in F.* Tamiris led her young group through a spirited performance of Whitman's *Salut au Monde.* Gluck Sandor was using the Prokofieff music for his new work, *The Eternal Prodigal.* Don Oscar Becque, head of the dance unit, was preparing *Young Tramps,* youths on the roads of America, to a new score by Donald Pond.

At the rambling scenic studio facing the noisy Sixth Avenue El, where the train screeched into Third Street, I spoke with Cleon Throckmorton, rotund friend of Eugene O'Neill, Susan Glaspell, James Light, and others of the *avant-garde* theatre in Greenwich Village. Throck was a soft-spoken man who was known in theatre circles for making scenery for shoestring producers and often not collecting a dime from them. Flanagan sought Throck's advice on sets for early pro-

50

Act Two

ject shows; and she asked him to devise a portable stage to present free shows in the city parks. When I saw him he was fixing up an old truck with switchboard, scenic equipment, and collapsable stage, setting up the first unit of the Caravan Theatre for $225.

Around the corner on Macdougal Street was the small Provincetown Playhouse, where Madalyn O'Shea was instructing teachers in all phases of stage production. When I first saw the theatre it had worn benches, a tiny stage, and a telephone-booth-size box office. In the basement crews took turns sewing costumes, painting scenery, and making props. Upstairs a technical crew worked the lights and arranged the cyclorama; others were reading scripts of Lynn Riggs' *Cherokee Night* and James Bridie's *Tobias and the Angel.* The training they received there prepared them for positions as drama leaders in community and regional centers throughout the nation.

At the Field Artillery Armory in Brooklyn, one of the biggest in the country, the Federal Theatre Circus played to 14,000, mostly children, for a dime. Of the three hundred in the company, half were performers, sixty were in the circus band, and the rest were technicians and managerial staff. The circus also started on FERA and CWA, but Federal Theatre added variety and vaudeville to compensate for the few trained animal acts. After all, the aim of the project was to put actors, not elephants, back to work.

Some performers were headliners who had played before royalty and earned a thousand a week. A favorite was the "Strongest Woman in the World," who could bend a seven-foot rod as though it were a mammoth paperclip. A five-high pyramid act brought excited sighs when the top man jumped down to safety. There were the usual acts: trampoline, hand-balancing, daredevil cyclists, high and low wire walkers, single and double trapeze. (A horizontal bar acrobat was Burt Lancaster, who toured the New York and New Jersey WPA circuit.) The red-coated windjammers waltzed through many acts, but switched to fast tempos when the clowns burst into the arena for their comedy walkaround.

There Were No Elephants on Relief

*But 400,000 children have enjoyed the
Federal Theatre Circus anyway*

by Anthony Buttitta

More than 400,000 children of greater New York have been thrilled by the death-defying feats of aerialists, trick cyclists and tightwire walkers; have laughed and guffawed at the antics of 40 clowns -- from the world's smallest scaramouche to the tallest -- and have sung to the music of the biggest (positively!) circus band in the world, all part of the WPA Circus, a division of the Federal Theatre Project for New York City.

Organized at the beginning of the project, the circus gave its first performance on October 17, 1935, at the 2nd Naval Battalion Armory, Brooklyn. Up to May 1, 1936, it had played 106 times, to audiences totaling well over half a million -- counting adults.

But adults hardly count, as far as this unit of Federal Theatre is concerned. It was created for the youngest generation, and has on its program everything the youthful entertainment seeker expects of a circus. Everything, that is, except wild animals. But the absence of tigers, elephants and giraffes, wild men from Borneo and glass-eating freaks is scarcely noticed by the children. Most of them have never seen a circus; but even for those who

have, the 60 acts in the three-ring show are more than enough to keep them from missing the roar of the jungle beasts and the cracking whips of the trainers.

"The only reason we don't have elephants in this show is that none were on relief," Hallie Flanagan, national director of the Federal Theatre Project, said recently. Two trained ponies, a dozen dancing dogs and a pair of monkeys -- the property of certain performers on the project whose acts they constitute -- furnish enough animal interest in the show.

Asked if he missed the wild beasts, a 7-year-old Bronx boy replied, "I've seen the big stiffs at the zoo till I'm sick. I like the clowns lots better. They're the fun." Another boy answered that this was his first circus and that he was having plenty of fun with the clowns.

Clowns. That's the main attraction of the two and a half hour show. The two boys knew what they were talking about. Forty clowns -- many of them former big-top headliners on the major circuits here and abroad -- dance and tumble and buffoon in a series of walk-around interludes. From time to time, they

(From *Federal Theatre Magazine*, volume 1, number 6)

Act Two

Relief regulations were unfair to teams and animal acts. Only one member of a family, husband and wife or a sister act, was allowed on the project payroll. The owner of an animal act received a minimum salary, but no compensation for the service of his trained horse, pony, bear, dogs, or the mangy lion that was in the show. This was no doubt the reason why the Federal Theatre had no elephant at the time —the most popular symbol of a circus.

During my local tour of the project, I also investigated the sprawling unit of the Bureau of Research and Publications, which was on my floor at West 42nd Street. Its first director was Rosamond Gilder, whose responsibilities included the *Federal Theatre Magazine* as well as the National Play Bureau. When Miss Gilder returned to *Theatre Arts Monthly* a few months later, she was replaced by Kate Drain Lawson.

The Bureau was staffed by more than fifty men and women, young and old, who were reading, editing, writing, and translating plays. They made synopses and lists of plays too, and reported on them to project directors. They compiled original scripts for production by special units, made contracts with authors and agents, handled royalty payments and kept production records. They translated scripts into English and from English into foreign versions for Spanish, Jewish, Yiddish, and other languages.

With all this activity Miss Gilder and later Miss Lawson had little time to keep a close check on what Pierre de Rohan was doing with the *Federal Theatre Magazine.* And since Miss Lawson knew little about publications, he did as he wished. Though Flanagan had asked Mark and me to help raise its standard, I, as a newcomer, had still less chance to do so than Mark, who had preceded me by a few weeks.

10

MARCH also marked the official debut of the *Federal Theatre Magazine*, printed on the offset press in its new format. This issue was completely devoted to Flanagan's report on the first six months of the project, illustrated by two photographs and a regional map. It was an improvement over the *Bulletin,* but could have been more attractive and readable. Mark and I had made a dummy with a picture layout that would have broken up the pages of type. De Rohan saw otherwise; he made another one and left a blank page at the end—as if to remind us that he was running the magazine.

We all pitched in to collate the pages, staple, address, and mail bundles of copies to WPA officials, congressmen, critics, regional directors, and others on the project. It was free to all theatre workers, but most of them rarely saw or spoke of the magazine, as though it did not exist.

Afterwards, Mark and I discussed what strategy we should take in preparing the next issue. We agreed to fight strongly for more pictures and illustrations as well as a variety of features. He went to research what the other Arts projects were doing, and I finished my piece on "Dance Comes Back to the Theatre." We gave them to de Rohan, reminding him that Hallie had commissioned them, and included plenty of pictures. He scheduled them for the next number along with color reproductions of the Harlem *Macbeth* costume sketches.

Flanagan liked the start we had made but her attention was elsewhere. Censorship, which had plagued the project from the start, was constantly creating new problems as she made her field tours. She was pleased to see the red, white, and blue sign, *Work Pays America,* along with the WPA symbol, hanging over historic playhouses like the Walnut Street in Philadelphia, the Alcazar in San Francisco, and the Blackstone in Chicago. But her tours also confronted her with Americans who were angry, jealous, or resentful of Uncle Sam's attempt to revive the theatre. Mark and I read the reports as they filtered back to our office.

Hiram Motherwell, former editor of *Stage* and now regional director for the northeast, reported that "The newspapers down Boston way don't like us. One office has a sign on the reporters' call board: 'Soak the New Deal.' One of our plays in Cambridge called for a dog; the paper came out with the headline, 'Dog on Government Payroll.' We're about to do our first big show—*Valley Forge*. Don't think I've forgotten we're going heavy on history and the classics as well as straight entertainment. We're going to tour the play all over the state. . . . No experiments for New England."

When Maxwell Anderson's *Valley Forge* opened at Plymouth, Massachusetts, historic town of the early settlers, a selectman objected to its being unpatriotic and there was an uproar throughout the state. It was a successful Theatre Guild play, and the Federal Theatre production had been endorsed by Harvard professors, the president of the Watch and Ward Society, rector of the Emmanuel Church, president of the Massachusetts Historical Society, and a state commander of the American Legion.

Paul Edwards, state WPA administrator, at first supported the charges by saying, "The people of Massachusetts are going to have the type of plays they want. . . . If there is any scandal on the Federal Theatre project, I intend to get to the bottom of it." A week later he was quoted in the Boston *American* as saying, "I am perfectly satisfied that this is a lot of smoke with little fire." *Valley Forge* went on to play three towns; one of them was Concord, sponsored by the Women's Club. (Later it was learned that the patriotic selectman who started the uproar owned two movie houses in Plymouth.)

Censorship then spread to Connecticut, where New Britain citizens protested Shakespeare's *The Merchant of Venice* as being anti-Semitic. Regarding this Flanagan commented in

Arena: "If we couldn't produce patriotic American plays by famous American authors or classical masterpieces, what could we do for New England?" The answer was quick and to the point: the new state director announced *The First Year, The Patsy, The Spider, The Late Christopher Bean,* and *The Trial of Mary Dugan.*

While on the West Coast, Flanagan met Colonel Donald Connolly, WPA administrator for Southern California, who expressed his doubts about the Federal Theatre. When she asked his opinion of a good project, he replied: "One that keeps out of the papers." But the colonel was gracious enough—at the time—to bow out of the picture and let her run the project with Gilmor Brown and Howard Miller as her local directors. Since neither were of the commercial theatre, *Variety* reported that "little theatre people are getting all the breaks" on the theatre project.

In Minneapolis, 165 persons were eligible for the theatre project. Dale Riley, of the University of Minnesota drama department, who headed it, found that in this Midwest city of mixed nationalities there were a number of excellent actors of Scandinavian descent. Much of his audience was Norwegian, Danish, and Swedish; Riley set up, in addition to a program of modern plays, a repertory of Ibsen, Strindberg, and Bjørnson.

During the early auditions, the Minneapolis *Journal* printed a photograph of a fan dancer with the caption, "Federal Fan Dancer No. 1," as if to give the impression that this was the type of entertainment the WPA was presenting. The picture appeared in two New York City papers, the *Daily News* and the *Herald Tribune,* and in the Baltimore *Sun.* Despite denials by WPA officials in Minnesota and Washington and the dancer involved, the picture kept appearing in newspapers throughout the nation.

As it turned out, the dancer had worked several years before WPA in a night club, and the photograph was of that period. She was now on relief, had applied for a job with the Federal Theatre as a tap dancer, but was not at any time on it. The publicity created such an uproar that the state administrator shut down the Minneapolis project—before a curtain had gone up—and 165 eligible professionals were thrown out of work.

But there were also dozens of bright moments when Flanagan realized that she was indeed touching the people. Oklahoma had a theatre for the blind with two on the payroll, a director and his assistant. Actors were students of the Oklahoma School for the Blind; their scripts were transcribed in Braille and memorized. And in Nebraska she wrote us of a performance of Richard Harding Davis' *The Dictator*, presented in a school house. Eight hundred people tried to get in to see the first production. It was toured by the Omaha unit, which estimated that ninety percent of the audience had never seen a live show before anywhere. After the performance, Hallie watched dozens of people waiting to see and touch the actors to make sure they had seen "real people."

11

PROSPERO
Now does my project gather to a head:
My charms crack not; my spirits obey . . .
How's the day?

ARIEL
On the sixth hour; at which time, my lord,
You said our work should cease.

PROSPERO
I did say so
When I rais'd the tempest.

MARK and I found these words in the opening of act five of *The Tempest,* which we saw performed by the classical unit on the subway circuit. They seemed as prophetic in relation to the Federal Theatre as the feats of wizardry that Prospero in his magic robes conjured up on the stage. Hallie was our conjurer whose "charms crack not" and her "spirits obey"; she "rais'd the tempest"—many a tempest—with a kind of theatre that was putting actors back to work in hundreds of shows to entertain a vast American audience.

A day or so after we saw the play, a tall, light-footed young man with blond hair falling over his boyish face breezed into Room 410, the magazine office, with a manila envelope under his arm. After a quick "Hi," he opened the bulging envelope and showed us a batch of charcoal and pencil sketches he had made of Federal Theatre shows. One of the drawings was of Prospero, wearing a crown and his robes, surrounded by the sprite Ariel and guards, as he looked at the audience through a partly drawn curtain from the wings—just as we sometimes did to check the house from backstage. It bore the line: "Now does my project gather to a head."

Now does my project gather to a head.
(Shakespeare, *The Tempest*)

"You're Don Freeman," I said, recognizing his lively and playful style. "I've seen your stuff in the Sunday *Trib.*"

"Luck—with all the freelancers hot-footing it there and to the *Times,*" he said.

"Just what we need," Mark said as he leafed through them, "to brighten things up here."

"You're welcome to them."

"We can't pay."

"I'm on the Art project," Don replied, pulling a sketch pad from his pocket. "I'm gutting the market."

"We certainly can use some," I ventured. "But we'll have to show them to de Rohan."

"No rush."

"Maybe it's better if Don shows them," Mark said to me. "If we push them, he might balk. Don, go see de Rohan. The press room down the hall."

That morning I proofed "The Dance Comes Back to the Theatre," which was set for the upcoming number of the magazine. When Don looked in a few minutes later to say that de Rohan had taken three drawings and was using the Prospero one in the same issue, I left with him to have a cup of coffee.

As he steered me toward Times Square, Don told me he was from San Diego; he had recently come to New York to study with John Sloan at the Art Students League. He had started out playing a horn to support himself; he had played at weddings and *festas* from the Bronx to the Lower East Side, and in such night spots as El Chico in Sheridan Square, where he had to wear the gaucho uniform of the band.

One day Don left his horn in the subway and his musical career took second place; he did not have the money to buy another one. Turning to his sketching talent he began to roam all over town—parks, subways, the Bowery, the theatre district—sketching whatever caught his fancy to record the pulsating life of the big city. His first drawing to appear in the *Herald Tribune* was a bustling scene in Shubert Alley at intermission time, when actors of the two theatres mingled with the audience.

Act Two

Thousands of jobless artists and actors had tramped the city streets, but with his horn Don had earned enough to send for his bride, Lydia Cooley, to join him in the flat on 14th Street, which he had chosen for their delayed honeymoon. Lydia was an artist too; she sketched, painted, and did miniature sculptures. But Don's freelance earnings were so irregular that he was eligible for a job on the Art project. This made it possible for him to study lithography and printmaking at the League; he later issued collections of his sketches and drawings as *Don Freeman's Newsstand.*

"Would you like to switch to our project?" I asked him in the Automat on Times Square. "You could do plenty for us."

"Be great."

Before we left, he told me that he had lived for weeks on a thirty-cent meal there of baked beans, rolls, apple pie, and coffee. At the corner of 44th Street, Don excused himself and turned into Whalen's to make a call. I soon learned that it was a hangout for theatre people to telephone, swap show-biz gossip, and get tips on casting, passes to shows, and sometimes a party with good food.

Though Don did nothing about my suggestion, it was in line with the policy of the four Arts projects. Many artists painted signs, created posters, and designed in the scenic shops. Writers were assigned to the research bureau and the Living Newspaper. The music project not only assigned musicians for theatre orchestras and musicals, but had the theatre project join it in its presentation of Ernst Toch's *The Princess on the Pea,* a modern comic opera freely adapted from the Andersen fairy tale that later inspired a popular musical, *Once Upon a Mattress.*

While waiting outside Whalen's, I watched the passing crowd at the corner of 42nd Street and Broadway. I saw a familiar sign: Central Ticket Agency, which was in the basement of Gray's Drugstore. It was operated by Joe Leblang, a legendary Broadway figure who had saved many shows from *Abie's Irish Rose* to *The Greenwich Village Follies* with his cut-rate ticket business. (While at Chapel Hill in the early thirties, I had come up to see shows; without Leblang's I

To Tony, my crony (no baloney) Don Freeman
(Courtesy of Margo Feiden Galleries)

could not have seen Judith Anderson in Pirandello's *As You Desire Me.*)

Leblang started peddling tickets on Herald Square before the theatres moved up to Times Square, leaving the 34th Street area to department stores like Macy's. In those days Herald Square was like a midway: brokers sold tickets out of their derbies and cigar boxes instead of a hole in the wall. Some were scalpers with hot tickets, some were sidewalk hawkers peddling ordinary tickets at reduced prices shortly before curtain time as crowds descended on the square to see a show that cost no more than a first-run movie.

"Ever see the line around that corner?" Don asked when he came out. He pointed to the 45th Street corner at Loew's State Theatre. "The Actors' Dinner Club. Fed hundreds of actors in the basement. But it's gone out of business with Federal Theatre."

As Don led me up Broadway to the Manhattan Theatre, where he was going to sketch the box office line for *Murder in the Cathedral,* he told me about the club. It was founded in the early thirties by Equity and other theatrical unions to provide dinners for jobless members of their professions. By now more than 4,000 theatre people were on the New York City project, with a goal of 7,000 before the end of 1936.

"Know who those birds are?" Don asked as he pulled out a pad to sketch the ticket line that stretched up Broadway.

"No," I said, looking at the straggled queue of men and women, chatting and reading newspapers.

"Diggers."

That was the word for people hired by agencies to buy tickets for hot shows—if they could not get them from managers and producers for their customers. The Federal Theatre had a policy of not dealing with brokers; all tickets were sold at the box office, except theatre parties for various organizations. When *Murder* became a sellout, the box office sale was limited to two pairs per person. This made it difficult for agencies; they had to keep sending diggers to take care of their customers.

"If you think this is something," Don said, as he sketched

a woman in the line wearing a shabby fox piece, "scoot up to Harlem and see what it's like for the *Macbeth* opening."

When I reached the Lafayette, I learned that opening night had been sold out for almost a week. Scalpers buzzed around the Seventh Avenue bars that flanked the theatre, selling tickets at prices higher than the Eliot play. I saw truckloads of heavy scenery, Napoleonic uniforms with gold braid, and gorgeous satin gowns, all designed by Nat Karson, being delivered to the theatre. Inside the company of a hundred was being directed by Orson Welles. The large orchestra was rehearsing the Virgil Thomson waltzes for the lavish ball scene, and Feder was spotting a battery of lights to work his magic on the witches' scene.

About four days before the premiere, Harlem discovered MACBETH stenciled in luminous letters on street corners from 120th to 140th streets between Lexington and Broadway. Two nights later a dress rehearsal was thrown open to project people and friends. Police were called to hold back an estimated 3,000 trying to crash after the house had exceeded the capacity fixed by the fire department.

The crowd more than tripled but was orderly on April 14, when *Macbeth* opened to the fanfare and the excitement of a Hollywood premiere. Two bands of the Order of Elks, dressed in snappy blue, scarlet, and gold uniforms, marched up and down Seventh Avenue with flying banners of "Macbeth by Wm. Shakespeare" and converged on the Lafayette eighty-five strong with martial sounds. Traffic was snarled. Police held back crowds to clear the way for taxis and limousines rolling up with celebrities, critics, and WPA officials. Flashbulbs popped and newsreel cameras were set up on a truck to catch the first-nighters flashing jewels, silk hats, ermine, and silver minks.

I was lucky to have seen the dress rehearsal; I had no opening night ticket. Flanagan was there wearing her usual corsage. She considered Houseman and Welles her two most original showmen; their voodoo *Macbeth* delighted her with its backdrop of the world's largest skeleton arch, its African drum beat, and "jungle throbbing with sinister life." The

Act Two

cheering lasted fifteen minutes. Atkinson wrote in the *Times:* "*Macbeth* merited the excitement that rocked the Lafayette theatre last night." Another critic described the show as "a tragedy of black ambition in a green jungle shot through with such lights from heaven and hell as no other stage has seen."

The critics were in a mood to praise—all but the venerable Percy Hammond, critic at the *Herald Tribune.* This brief excerpt from his report the following morning sounded more like a review of the New Deal than the show he had seen: "The Negro Theatre, an offshoot of the Federal Government and one of Uncle Sam's experimental philanthropies, gave us last night an exhibition of deluxe boondoggling."

Our African drummers, resentful of his remarks, had a powwow and decided to take care of the man. We soon learned that they remained in the theatre after the evening performances and beat out voodoo in a candle-lit wing of the basement, calling on their gods to punish the critic. A few days later Percy Hammond was stricken with pneumonia and died—before he could hear that Charles B. Cochran, the London producer, had cabled for exclusive rights to present our voodoo *Macbeth* in the British Isles.

12

In the spring of 1936, while Harry Hopkins was preparing to testify before the House Appropriations Committee, Mark was teaching me to "eat like a New Yorker." I preferred the automats where you could dine quickly and well for a few nickles, and we sampled the offerings along 42nd Street, later branching out to my favorite on West 23rd. Mark also took me to Thompson's, those thrifty cafeterias with the restaurant-like atmosphere where you could get a full meal for a quarter and pie, in season, for another nickle. I haunted a small Coney Island "stand-up" off Broadway where a tiny, grey man carefully placed mustard, chili, and onions on my hot dog and then delivered it with a smile and cup of coffee for ten cents. Sometimes we stood in line behind a counter stool at the "five and dime" awaiting a "blue-plate" special of meat loaf, mashed potatoes, and beans for 25 cents. A nickle was a valuable thing and sometimes the lines were long.

They were heady times. After all with *Murder in the Cathedral, Chalk Dust, Triple-A Plowed Under,* and *Macbeth* all playing to full houses in New York City, Uncle Sam was emerging as the greatest producer since Flo Ziegfeld. But our joy was not shared by everyone, especially those congressmen hostile to Roosevelt and the New Deal. For them—the diehard Republicans and Southern Democrats—relief should be charity not work, especially work in something as trivial as the theatre. For us, work-relief was central to restoring people's morale as well as utilizing their talent.

The real fear of some congressmen that spring of 1936 was that the Roosevelt administration was using WPA relief funds to keep itself in power by winning over the American people. The Federal Theatre, in particular, they suspected, was being used to showcase the principles of the New Deal, principles which to certain lawmakers smacked of Socialism and Communism.

In April, Representatives Bacon, Woodrum, and other members of the Appropriations Committee finally got to grill Harry Hopkins about the political activities of the Federal Theatre. Jane Mathews reports that Bacon, the Long Island Republican who had denounced *Triple-A* as "pure, unadulterated propaganda," said that he had received complaints from a Veterans group that the play was propaganda. And Woodrum, the conservative Virginia Democrat, called *Triple-A* a "Gridiron Club proposition."

Hopkins pointed out that it was neither. He described the historical content of the production and compared it to a dramatized version of the news. And he further stressed that the play was good and effective theatre and suggested that those who were attacking *Triple-A* should first go and see it, as a test perhaps of their own perceptions. Think of it, he urged, as something like *March of Time* in the movies.

Representative Bacon pursued the argument that, in an election year, it was important that taxpayers' money, meant for relief, should not be used for political purposes by the Federal Theatre. Hopkins defended the project, saying that the sort of people managing it would not tolerate "identification with any kind of enterprise that was of a partisan propaganda nature, and nothing like that will be permitted . . . in terms of the type of propaganda you are thinking of."

Along with other New Dealers, Hopkins believed that Federal Theatre propaganda directed toward a better life for more people was good propaganda for American democracy. This idea served to counteract left-wing agitation during the Depression for reforms that would lead to such a life. WPA projects were set up to employ the skills and talents of dispossessed millions, many of whom had been calling for a revolution. Thus the New Deal did not change the capitalist system, as its loudest critics declared, but saved it along with American democracy.

Mathews also describes how a few days later Senator

Uncle Sam Presents

James Davis, a Pennsylvania Republican, told the Senate that the Roosevelt administration was allowing money meant for relief to be spent by a woman who had spoken in glowing terms of the Russian theatre and the Soviet Union. Launching into what he called "a sordid chapter in American history," the senator read from letters sent him by the Federal Theatre Veterans League and an Equity member speaking of Communists on the New York City project.

Senator Davis then read passages from *Shifting Scenes, Can You Hear Their Voices?* and other Flanagan writings. He stated that nowhere did she have a "good word to say about the economic system" which made possible relief money for WPA projects. He clinched his remarks with a quote from *Shifting Scenes:* "I became absorbed by the drama outside the theatre, the strange and glorious drama that is Russia."

"Why was such a woman appointed to administer over $7,000,000 of relief money?" asked Senator Davis. "Why was relief money, intended to feed hungry people, being used for such alien and subversive purposes?"

These questions and what they implied were printed by the press throughout the nation. But the same press buried remarks by Senator Robert Wagner, New York Democrat, when he read on the Senate floor telegrams from New York project officials and Frank Gillmore, Equity president, repudiating the charges. Flanagan also denied that she was interested only in the Russian theatre and its methods of production. She then dropped the matter and let the project record of successes be her best defense.

That spring Flanagan was not sure whether the Federal Theatre would continue nationally after the current funds ended June 30. President Gillmore warned Equity that the projects might be turned over to the states again; he sent fifty telegrams to New York congressmen in Washington and called Chicago and Los Angeles Equity heads to protest this probable action to their congressmen. They were joined by protests from the American Federation of Musicians and the International Alliance of Theatrical and Stage Employees (IATSE).

Act Two

Variety claimed that the locals of seven hundred stage-hand unions sent telegrams to Washington. Later, in reporting that combined pressure was behind the project, the showbiz journal warned that the congressional fight would not be won until attempts to earmark funds had been defeated. When the fight resumed on Capitol Hill, Republicans and Southern Democrats charged the WPA with the usual complaints of extravagance and radicalism.

On May 11, the appropriations bill passed the House without funds being earmarked and the Federal Theatre was saved. Flanagan wired her regional directors that the project would live another year. But during the skirmish in the House she had met the enemy face to face. At first they poked fun at the project and laughed at the idea that we could put on a show. Now that we were a resounding success, they changed their tactics to redden our name with cries of propaganda and radicalism. The coalition of malcontents, Veterans, superpatriots, and hired spies had nearly destroyed the project, but we had survived.

Mark and I celebrated at the Automat on 42nd Street. Considering the strength of the opposition, it was a victory for the Federal Theatre to win funds for another year. But we soon learned that the forces opposed to a genuine people's theatre were not defeated but only more determined than ever.

13

THE April issue of the magazine appeared at the end of the month. It was delayed because of the time required to process the color reproductions of the *Macbeth* costume sketches. Don Freeman's drawing, backstage at *The Tempest,* faced the Report on Federal Theatre activities. With the color pages, Don's black and white, layouts of audience and production shots, and articles on various units, the magazine moved up alongside the best theatre publications of the time.

This was the only number to carry a complete masthead. Mark, Portner, and I were listed as reporters, a typist as editorial assistant, and Pierre de Rohan as editor. The artist, secretary, and pressmen were also mentioned. Afterwards, the only name to appear was that of de Rohan as editor, and occasionally some assistant—for what reason we never learned.

The artist Alice Fried had drawn a statistical chart showing the percentages of workers on the project: 47 percent actors, 14 percent stagehands and technicians, 5 percent directors, 3 percent writers, and 2 percent artists; the remainder consisted of ushers, clerks, and watchmen. The chart followed Flanagan's piece, "Men at Work: South," summarizing a two-week tour of southern projects with emphasis on North Carolina, Florida, and Louisiana.

Byline pieces on the other Arts projects were by Mark, the marionette theatre by Portner, the play bureau by Gilder, my article on the dance unit, and an unsigned resume on how the Living Newspaper was put together. A page at the back reprinted letters, "Curtain Calls by Mail," praising Federal Theatre shows, from teachers, professors, social workers, Red Cross, Masonic Home, and the American Legion.

De Rohan commented on productions in a tone that was

sometimes as sarcastic as that of George Jean Nathan in the Hearst *Journal-American*. On his "Box Score" page was a reprint of the Robert Benchley comment from *The New Yorker:* "A new and rather exciting element has crept into the New York theatrical season. . . . All over town, from Harlem to Macdougal Street, little theatre groups of hitherto unemployed actors, musicians, and technicians are putting on shows, under the auspices of the Federal government, and darned good shows, too. . . . The five I have seen would have been definitely worth doing, which is more than I can say for five consecutive shows on Broadway."

While Flanagan was busy saving the project, a variety of activities kept us busy that spring. Federal Theatre of the Air made its debut without fanfare. Using professional actors for whom there were no shows, it broadcast a weekly series, "Professional Parade." The series was produced by Evan Roberts, head of the radio unit, with Fred Niblo, the well-known director of silent films, as master of ceremonies introducing the cast of actors to the radio audience.

During the early months of the project, Flanagan had gotten Roberts to prepare a plan for the radio unit to show Washington officials. They turned it down, saying that it was impossible; Washington could not buy or get free time, and besides no government bureau could go on the air. But having learned how to get things done the bureaucratic way, she had Roberts show the plan to CBS and NBC network officials.

With actors, directors, writers, and technicians available on project rolls, the networks would be getting shows that cost them nothing but radio time—and they had plenty of it those days to spare. After setting up a studio with improvised equipment, Flanagan persuaded WPA officials to let them give the project a try. From the first show, Federal Theatre of the Air was successful; it was soon releasing programs through regular radio channels and the three networks NBC, CBS, and Mutual, with no advertising. This in a way was the forerunner of what is known today as national public, noncommercial radio.

When the limited engagement of *Murder in the Cathedral*

ended, we lost the Manhattan. Flanagan appealed to the League of New York Theatres and was allowed to lease four dark houses from the Shuberts. The Adelphi on West 53rd replaced the Manhattan; the Ritz on West 49th Street was for the Children's Theatre; the Maxine Elliott on West 39th Street for Houseman and Welles' new classical unit Project #891; and the small Nora Bayes over the 44th Street Theatre for dance productions.

Macbeth was slated to tour Hartford, Detroit, Cleveland, Indianapolis, Chicago, Dallas, and three other cities after it was moved for a downtown engagement to make way for a new Negro Theatre play at the Lafayette. Houseman left the unit in charge of his assistant, Carlton Moss, and Gus Smith, whose play *Turpentine* was scheduled to open there. It was a drama of protest exposing the injustice of the southern labor-camp system in the pine forests. As it had none of the exotic or classic splendor of *Macbeth,* the Negro middle-class community stayed away from it. Monroe Burnett, who handled Negro press for the unit, told me that theatre-going Harlem did not like to see themselves depicted in what they dubbed "overall plays."

From May until fall, when Broadway producers took to the summer theatres of barns in the nearby hills, the New York City project launched a steady production schedule. *Backwash,* another Managers' try-out play, was sold to Broadway for the fall opening. And *We Live and Laugh,* a Yiddish revue with native folk tunes and humor was a popular success at the Public Theatre. Mark took Hallie and me down to Second Avenue so he could translate bits of dialog and songs for us. *Variety* said that it gave "The Yiddish theatre its first taste of a revue on a big scale."

A new edition of the Living Newspaper replaced *Triple-A* at the Biltmore on May 12. It was *Highlights of 1935,* researched and written by the staff, with H. Gordon Graham as production director. The script was not controversial; it simply presented news without a point of view. The events involved a group of average Americans on the jury in the Hauptmann-Lindberg trial. Despite some effective scenes, it was the least exciting edition and I have no memory whatever of it.

Class of '29 by Orrie Lashin and Milo Hastings was a production of the Popular Price Theatre. When it opened on May 15, we were surprised that it alarmed some superpatriots on the project. It was a realistic indictment of unemployment as it affected four Harvard graduates in the class of 1929. Reviewing it in the *Times,* Atkinson said that it would be good for congressmen to see it so they might learn that "the thinking of young college graduates is very intimately influenced by the treatment they receive at the hands of business and the government." The play was duplicated in Boston, Los Angeles, Denver, and eight other cities.

The final show of the project's first Broadway season was *Battle Hymn,* which opened May 22, as an Experimental Theatre offering. It was written by Michael Gold and Michael Blankfort, well-known left-wing writers, and staged by the young director, Vincent Sherman. It told the story of John Brown, the abolitionist, who made a dramatic attempt to end slavery with his fiery stand at Harper's Ferry. Though de Rohan in his box score made what Flanagan considered "a snappish remark" when he said that the project at last had "convictions," Archer Winston wrote in the *Post,* "I'd rather miss any show in New York than this one."

With the end of the first production season Federal Theatre, by using less money and more ingenuity as a relief project, had done as good a job as the best Broadway producer. By now over 12,000 persons were working in 158 theatres in twenty-eight states, and playing to a combined weekly audience of a half-million. Without having attempted to reproduce the old commercial theatre of escape or to save the road, Uncle Sam had started a new kind of theatre—a theatre of adventure that gave audiences what they wanted in the way of entertainment and at a price they could afford to pay.

14

THAT weekly audience of a half-million did not include the thousands of youths who saw Federal Theatre shows touring hundreds of Civilian Conservation Corps camps. Nor did it include such pageants as the Houston tribute to the Lone Star State or the 40,000 who attended the *America Sings* spectacle in the huge Little Rock amphitheatre. Against a shimmering background of the sunny Arkansas sky, the history of the Southwest under five flags swept across the vast open-air stage set up in the capital for the Centennial event.

Reports and photographs reached our office from all the projects and Mark and I would immediately check the material for something to use in the magazine. Some of it came to us direct, some first went to Flanagan or to the research bureau and was relayed to us. De Rohan was no longer pleased with the kind of photographs we were getting even from the New York units so we scoured the mails. That summer there was a great deal from the Southwest.

June 10, 1936, was President's Day in Arkansas, a state friendly to the New Deal. The State Centennial Committee, WPA agencies, Federal Theatre and the Music Project, civic and educational groups, were joined by 16,000 participants who came to honor the President of the United States. John McGee, southern regional director, Fred Morrow, and others wrote and produced the pageant.

The people of Arkansas cheered the President and banners waved in the street: "Arkansas Welcomes the President!" At Hot Springs his car moved slowly alongside a mass of people, clapping, shouting, and waving flags. At Rockport, where the President spoke in a small country church, Negroes lined the streets wearing flowers and feathers in their hair. It was hot but the President and Mrs. Roosevelt were relaxed, happy, and carefree.

Look, Spike, now they're coming
to the obligatory scene.

Uncle Sam Presents

The scene was repeated in Texas—heat, people lining the street, flowers and flags, speeches, cheering and applause. Using the Alamo as a backdrop, F.D.R. spoke to an enthusiastic audience. Later, from the back of the car, he addressed a large group under a huge electric sign, "The Rose of Prosperity Blooms Again in Roosevelt." The spirit of the Southwest was summarized in the Arkansas pageant: "Let us hold to the splendid courage of the pioneer spirit that would not quit. Let us keep faith in ourselves and in our country."

Meanwhile in New York City I attended a preview of the *CCC Murder Mystery,* a comedy by Grace Heyward which was produced especially for about 300,000 youths in 258 CCC camps throughout the nation. As a guest of camp officials, the author researched her play on the spot and wrote it with a CCC volunteer at each camp involved in the mystery. The plot also called for his friend's participation. In the mess hall they watched the play unfold while sitting on tables, window sills, and the floor.

The jurors (boys and officers of the post) were chosen and sworn in, and then witnesses were called. Eight actors in the touring company, with no scenery and with only a few hand props, carried the burden of the play. In this way the trial of one of their own camp members, accused of murder, was presented. As an early experiment in audience participation, it was praised by *Variety* for its "naturalness and pungency lacking in orthodox productions." The murder mystery was toured to camps by companies from New York City, Boston, Philadelphia, and other cities.

While New York producers planned next season or basked in the cool of Skowhegan, Bar Harbor, and Newport, we at Federal Theatre kept busy with new shows. July brought additional successes: *Help Yourself,* a farce by Paul Vulpius, and *Injunction Granted,* another controversial edition of the Living Newspaper. *Help Yourself* was presented by Edward Goodman at the Adelphi; it was based on a Chaplin-like situation of an unemployed young man who hangs his hat in a big bank where he has no job and takes over as an expert in an imaginary land deal. The role was played by Curt Bois, a young Viennese actor, and it had a long run. It eventually was done in twenty-one other cities.

Injunction Granted, written by the Living Newspaper staff, was a history of the American labor movement and the unfair treatment it had received in the federal courts. Flanagan attended the premiere with Mrs. Ellen S. Woodward, new head of Federal One, and other WPA officials from Washington. They all praised the show, but it struck Flanagan as "bad journalism and hysterical theatre." She quickly passed on her reaction to Morris Watson, the producer, and Joe Losey, the director, adding that she noticed they had made changes since the last rehearsal, and that these changes damaged the play as drama and weakened its impact as documented theatre.

Watson, ignoring her criticism, replied that *Injunction Granted* was drawing big crowds. To quote from *Arena,* she

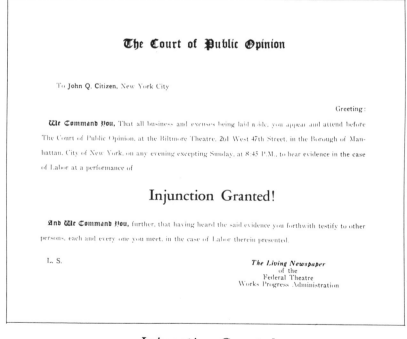

Injunction Granted

told him box office was not their prime aim and concluded, "Morris, I want you and Joe to be clear about this. As I have repeatedly said, I will not have the Federal Theatre used politically. I will not have it used to further the ends of the Democratic Party, the Republican Party, or the Communist Party." They made the necessary changes, but serious political damage had been done—as we were to learn later.

But one event that we were anticipating most that summer did not arrive until September—the premiere of Houseman's and Welles' Project #891. Hallie had recently acquired the Maxine Elliott Theatre, which had been built at the turn of the century by J. P. Morgan, to house the unit; and Welles with Edwin Denby was preparing a raucous adaptation of *The Italian Straw Hat* called *Horse Eats Hat.*

Many talents were involved in this production besides Welles and Denby, who were also in the cast. Welles played the bride's father and Denby was half of the horse that eats the hat. Houseman produced it but gave Welles a free hand; Nat Karson designed the lavish costumes and decor; Paul Bowles wrote the score; and Virgil Thomson orchestrated it and also chose authentic period rolls for the mechanical piano.

The cast was studded with names that were to shine on Broadway and in Hollywood. In addition to Welles, playing opposite his wife Virginia as the bride, there was Joseph Cotten as the harassed bridegroom, Hiram Sherman as the bride's cousin, Paula Lawrence, a dallying wife, and Arlene Francis as Tillie, owner of the hat shop. The show had a large cast, a full orchestra in the pit, and other musicians playing onstage.

Houseman in his memoir *Run-Through* described a bit of its artful lunacy: "Madness followed madness through the crowded acts—with actors by the score hurtling across the stage . . . in endless circular pursuit, in carriages and cars, tricycles and roller skates, walking, trotting, galloping, like a herd of hysterical elephants, leaving ruin in their wake . . . . I can still see Joe Cotten . . . leaping from sofa to table to piano top to chandelier in a wild, forty-foot flight till he vanished in the flyloft, while a three-tiered fountain flung a giant stream upward at the seat of his pants and Cotten himself . . . squirting streams of soda water over the madly whirling crowd below."

What impressed me most about this Wellesian frolic was not so much the demented action as the fast-moving sets, the lavish costumes, and the carnival-like musicians on a spree. There was a set of seven doors for playing hide and seek, reminiscent of chases in silent films; furniture that was designed to collapse on cue for zany business; and that swinging chandelier right out of Johann Strauss. Musicians were everywhere: in the pit, on the stage, backstage, in the boxes, and a strolling gypsy band. At intermission, a mechanical piano pumped out old melodies in a box while in the opposite box a tall woman wearing a hussar's uniform played a waltz on a trumpet. It was a five-ring circus: I had seen nothing like it at the Hippodrome, Barnum & Bailey, or in a Cecil B. de Mille film.

Cue wrote that *Horse Eats Hat* was "close to being a work of genuine theatre art . . . played in a tempo that leaves art, life, audience, and sometimes the actors behind it. A demented piece of surrealism." Louis Nichols in the *Times:* "It apparently didn't mean anything at all . . . had no beginning and no end and lacks rhyme and reason." John Chapman described it in the *Daily News* as "a continual state of explosive disintegration." Though critics and audiences were baffled by Welles' personal joke, *Horse Eats Hat* was embraced by the elegant theatre crowd and became a fashionable Broadway hit.

While this hilarity went on nightly at the Maxine Elliott, the Popular Price Theatre was rehearsing a new drama about the rising threat of fascism, not in Europe but in America. It was a dramatization of Sinclair Lewis' best-selling novel *It Can't Happen Here*, for which MGM had paid $200,000 for the screen rights and then shelved for fear that it might offend Hitler and Mussolini. It was planned for late October as a Federal Theatre coup to mark the first anniversary of the project. The premiere would take place in eighteen key cities from New York to Los Angeles on the same night—an event never before or since attempted in the theatre world.

15

IF Sinclair Lewis had not been married at the time to Dorothy Thompson, the politically-oriented journalist, he might not have written *It Can't Happen Here.* This was first told me by Louis Adamic, his friend and a contributing editor of *Contempo,* who had furnished Lewis with the labor background for his novel *Ann Vickers.* It was confirmed by Lewis when I met him at a New York hotel. At that meeting I used the occasion to thank him personally for the twenty-five dollar check which had accompanied a letter he wrote me during the difficult time of the controversial Scottsboro issues of the magazine.

It was Thompson who, after a stint of covering Europe for American newspapers, made him aware of the rise of fascism and what Hitler and Mussolini were doing to swallow their neighbors while the democracies looked on confused and helpless. When they discussed the fascist pair, he called them "clowns," and he referred to the European situation scornfully as "it." Lewis changed his tune when he realized that the menace could reach America in the guise of radical reformers, conservative politicians, and rabble-rousing superpatriots. These groups all raised their voices to "save" the country from the social and economic upheaval brought on by the Depression.

The menace of fascism emerged with the mushrooming of demagogic figures and such groups as America First, the Liberty League, and the Veterans' League. Topping the demagogues was Senator Huey P. Long, "Kingfish" ex-governor of Louisiana with his Share the Wealth program. Gerald L. K. Smith was starting the American Nazi Party, backed by Governor Eugene Talmadge of Georgia, whose political and racial policies were overtly fascist. Father Charles Coughlin, the Detroit radio priest, was on the air with his anti-Semitic slogans.

There were incidents already that smacked of the rising menace. In Indiana a presidential candidate was jailed a few weeks before the November elections. A permit was refused to a Major General of the Marines to speak before the League Against War and Fascism. A Florida labor leader was murdered by a deputized mob. In Yorkville, New York City, Fritz Kuhn was organizing brown-shirted members into the German-American Bund to the Hitler Salute. In Asheville, William Dudley Pelley, head of the Silver Shirts, kept his Galahad Press busy printing Nazi propaganda to flood the nation.

Lewis was aware that American liberals, radicals, and fellow travelers, fearful that fascism could happen here, were forming a united front to stop the menace before it took over America as it had done Central Europe. They knew that Lewis was an outspoken anti-Communist, but did not mind as long as he was not for Hitler. *It Can't Happen Here,* as a best-selling novel, is believed to have done as much to arouse popular opinion against fascism in America as the combined agitation of liberal and radical groups since Mussolini and Hitler rose to haunt the Western world.

Metro-Goldwyn-Mayer bought the novel from typescript; it was published in late October 1935, and was an immediate best-seller. The novel was more of a news than a literary event, according to Mark Schorer, Lewis' biographer, and was greeted by critics and newsmen as a political act of the times. Not that it was such a courageous feat, but it was the first popular polemic on our homegrown variety of fascists, whom Lewis also referred to as "clowns." That summer Lewis was vacationing in Europe when he learned of Long's assassination; he cabled his publisher to change all references to the senator in the novel as "the late Huey Long."

In February, Lewis was told that MGM had abandoned the film of the book. Different reasons appeared in the press. Will Hays, Hollywood censor czar, banned it for fear of international repercussions on orders from the Republican Party. The Hays office later denied that it was halting the film, and

MGM announced that it could not risk the high production cost. Then an MGM official blamed it on casting problems. Later a bulletin from Germany and Italy approved the banning and called Lewis "a full-blooded Communist."

While the controversy kept the novel in the news and at the top of the best-seller list that summer of 1936, Flanagan met with the newly formed Play Policy Board in New York City. This group, operating within the frame of the old Bureau of Research, was composed of regional directors, heads of the New York City projects, directors and supervisors of producing units, and members of the Play Bureau. At this planning meeting Francis Bosworth, director of the bureau, said that Shakespeare hung like a dark cloud over the modern theatre.

Someone asked, "What would you do instead?"

"Why not get Sinclair Lewis to dramatize *It Can't Happen Here* and do the play all over the country?"

"Magnificent," said William Farnsworth, the Washington Federal One deputy, who was at the meeting. "And open it everywhere on the *same* night."

This plan clinched the deal and Lewis was approached for the rights to stage the novel. He hesitated, saying that his agent was dickering with offers from commercial producers, but the idea that it would be done live in eighteen key cities and at movie prices appealed to him. Contracts were drawn up and Lewis called in a Hollywood collaborator, John C. Moffitt, to help dramatize the novel. They went to Lewis' Vermont farm, where he drank more than he wrote; the pair then returned to New York, set themselves up in separate suites at the Essex House facing Central Park, and went to work on the script.

Flanagan, who was also staying at the hotel, tells in *Arena* part of the amusing and hectic story of what went on while Lewis and Moffitt wrote and rewrote scenes to the point that neither spoke to the other, and that she had to act as go-between. The harassed staff moved in and out of the suites of the warring writers, bringing typewriters, plenty of iced water and black coffee, and boxes of Fanny Farmer candy to keep Lewis on the wagon.

Act Two

Three members of the Play Bureau, Bosworth, his assistant
H. L. Fishel, and Converse Tyler of the play reading unit,
took turns with Lewis day and night. Fishel recently told me
that they were with the writer on different shifts; he or Bosworth during the day, and Tyler from around seven till eight
the next morning. Lewis wrote and rewrote scenes at all
hours; he read his efforts aloud to them for criticism and
suggestions, and then sat down to dash off a new dialogue
sequence. As he kept revising and rewriting, freshly written
scenes were rushed to the bureau to be typed and retyped,
and then forwarded to waiting directors throughout the
country, and to translators who were preparing foreign language versions.

Dorothy Thompson, who was living and working in her
East Side apartment, would show up at the suite while Lewis
and his companions worked frantically at the script. Unsure
of himself, Lewis would hand her a rough of his latest effort,
anxiously pacing the floor while awaiting her verdict.

"It stinks," was her usual comment, according to Fishel.

This infuriated Lewis; he would call her names and stalk
out of the suite. A few hours later he was back at the job.
Though this went on until almost opening day, Lewis took
time out to audition hundreds of actors for the Adelphi production. He read the script at the first rehearsal, playing all
the roles, and started directing the play. The job had been
assigned to Vincent Sherman, but he let Lewis take over at
first and they got along well. (Lewis chose Sidney Lumet,
who was then eleven, to play the boy; Lumet's father, a Yiddish actor, got on the project so that the future film director
could act in the play.)

Working closely with Sherman at rehearsals, Lewis one
day asked him, "Don't you think this play's terrible?"

"Yes."

Sherman told Professor Lorraine Brown, associate director
of the recently established Federal Theatre Research Center
at George Mason University, that he was surprised when
Flanagan gave him the Lewis play to direct. He had thought
she would assign it to Joe Losey who had worked with Lewis.

83

Uncle Sam Presents

Perhaps Flanagan was still annoyed by what Losey and Watson had done to the script of *Injunction Granted.*

The New York office had to cope with frantic telegrams from directors and unit managers everywhere. Denver: *Where is revised version act three Lewis play rush immediately.* Chicago: *New ending revised act three does not make sense please advise.* Tampa: *Spanish company cannot learn lines by October 27 unless full text received immediately.* San Francisco: *Object to cutting White House scene only good scene in Lewis play.* Los Angeles: *Making superhuman efforts to meet October 27 Lewis play stop imperative have no more revisions stop stop.*

Don Freeman and I watched the gathering storm with glee. Never had we seen a theatrical event cause so much furor. We sat at a back table in Kiernan and Dineen's, eating and drinking on credit, counting the headlines. I did not realize that I was a fledgling press agent, but I sensed that something extraordinary was happening. The nationwide press, which was also confused about the play, had given 78,000 lines of space to *It Can't Happen Here* before opening night. Some thought it aimed at helping to reelect President Roosevelt. Others that it was planned to defeat him. Some declared that the play was Communistic, others that it was New Deal, still others that it was fascist. But they all thought that its opening day—October 27—was involved with the coming November elections.

"Where the motion pictures feared to tread, Federal Theatre will step boldly into the limelight of a controversial issue," wrote the Hollywood *Citizen-Times.* The Hearst Los Angeles *Examiner* was indignant: "A novel so highly controversial and in such scabrous bad taste that it suffered rejection by all the important motion picture companies, *It Can't Happen Here* is now to be given nationwide staging under the gonfalon of the United States government itself. Propaganda—naked and unconcealed."

Theatre Arts Monthly praised the idea: "No other theatre in America would have the courage to offer *It Can't Happen Here* simultaneously in eighteen cities. A splendid method

Sinclair Lewis

Hallie Flanagan and Sinclair Lewis

for the playwright and the audience." The Worcester (Mass.) *Telegram:* "In these days there will always be those who regard any artistic achievement of a creative mind as propaganda. So far as Mr. Lewis' play about the United States going fascist is concerned, a majority of our citizens would agree that 'if this is propaganda make the most of it.'"

Brock Pemberton, the Broadway producer who kept himself in the limelight sniping at the project, now turned out to be a member of the National Committee of the Republican Party. Its presidential candidate in the November elections was his friend and fellow Kansan, Alf M. Landon. While *It Can't Happen Here* was in rehearsal, Pemberton announced to the press that the play was radical and, "It's funny to begin with, that the WPA can tackle something which the films cannot."

The Nation was quick to reply: "We think it's funny too, for different reasons . . . As for Mr. Pemberton's charge of radicalism . . . there is nothing to prevent him from putting on a rousing pro-fascist drama *It Can and Should Happen Here.*"

When I met Pemberton in the late forties as his press agent for the Joe E. Brown company of *Harvey,* I asked him about his attacks on the Federal Theatre and the Lewis play in particular. The laconic producer replied, "Politics."

16

TEN days before the premiere of *It Can't Happen Here*, Edward Goodman of the Popular Price Theatre asked Flanagan to postpone the New York City opening. The other cities might be regarded as tryout towns, he said, but this was Broadway. Commenting on Goodman's attitude, she later observed in *Arena:* "This was one of several times when I was furious with the provincialism of the New York project and its lack of any sense of the theatre we were trying to build. It seemed ironic that Omaha, Tampa, and every other small project struggling along with few resources could get the play on while New York, with practically unlimited people to choose from and shops to build in, continued to stall."

Sunday morning at ten, October 24, Sinclair Lewis telephoned Poughkeepsie: "Hallie, it's all terrible. Everybody's gone into a coma. I want you to get right on a train and come to New York and postpone the play a week and get new people to do everything, and do it yourself. . . . The living room on the stage looks like a cheap boarding house on Second Avenue. It is terrible. It is all a failure. . . ."

When Hallie reached the Adelphi, she joined Kate Drain Lawson, now a technical supervisor on the project, and two assistants in a huddle at the back of the theatre. Flanagan persuaded Lewis, Sherman, Tom Adrian Cracraft, the designer, and others to go to bed; then locking the theatre doors, she went to work with her emergency crew. Assisted by a few devoted stagehands, they set up, scene by scene, the realistic sets which had been bungled in the workshop. They spent the rest of the day rearranging, repainting, and redressing the sets.

Opening night at the Adelphi I watched the crowds coming to the theatre. It was nothing like the elegant *Macbeth* premiere in Harlem. There were a few celebrities, mostly friends of Lewis and Dorothy Thompson—Erika Mann and her husband, W. H. Auden, Ernst Toller, Roger Burlingame, Kurt Joos, Louis Adamic. Flashbulbs exploded. One of them caught Brock Pemberton as he looked at a poster in the Adelphi lobby.

I stood at the back with project friends. None of us had seats for the opening but this was an event we could not miss. Hallie chatted with Lewis before the houselights dimmed and they sat down. I thought of her big gamble: she did not think the play was a strong one, but it had a provocative idea and, as the audience listened, she was pleased to see that it was moved by Lewis' message of the possible rise of fascism in America.

During the first intermission Flanagan taxied over to the Biltmore to catch the second act of the Yiddish version. She did not understand a word, but watched the different styles of acting—this voluble and broad compared to the quiet performance at the Adelphi. The Yiddish version included scenes omitted from the other, notably that of the concentration camp. On the whole she thought it was a far better show. That same night the Suitcase Theatre production was playing in Staten Island, but she had no time to see it.

When she returned to the Adelphi, Flanagan found the lobby jammed; it was second intermission. She was greeted by Lee Shubert who said in his soft voice, "Critics won't like it, Mrs. Flanagan, but the audience does. It's in for a long run." Then, as the lights dimmed for the third act, Hallie stood on the steps at the back of the crowded house in front of Mark and me. I noticed that she watched the audience as much as the action on the stage.

The curtain fell to a dozen calls. There were cheers for Seth Arnold who played the liberal newspaper publisher, Doremus Jessup. Then there were cries of "Author! Author!" which Mark and I had a lot to do with starting. The tall, gaunt, awkward Lewis, who looked like a dolled-up scarecrow in his tuxedo, finally emerged on the stage. After the applause died down, there were calls for a speech. Lewis obliged the audience by pulling out his watch and saying, "I've been making a speech since 8:45."

That night Lewis and Dorothy Thompson gave a party at the Plaza for their friends and principals in the cast. I went along with Adamic. Lewis was in fine shape—at first—as Hallie handed him a batch of telegrams. Cleveland: *Responsive audience keying up performance applause after first act tremendous.* Detroit: *Audience enthusiasm mounting.* Indianapolis: *Capacity audience including Governor McNutt play received most enthusiastically.* Omaha: *Received with acclaim.* Boston: *Reception magnificent play will be popular success.*

After weeks of writing and rewriting, the uncertainty of what he was doing in a new field, the nibbling of chocolates while he was on the wagon, Lewis now let himself go as he sometimes did when he finished an arduous piece of work. He was in a mood to celebrate, and the telegrams Hallie gave him only served to make it a bangup celebration. He gathered friends around him and told Vincent Sherman that they were to collaborate on his new play, *For Us the Living,* which Sherman would direct. His voice got louder, his gestures broader, his words more reckless. Tall and gaunt, he was more like a scarecrow than the one I had seen on the stage. His wife tried to calm him; he grimaced and called her vile names. The shocked guests started to leave, paying their respects to her. With tears in her eyes, she was silent as they bade her good night—and the party was over.

The Broadway critics agreed with Richard Watts who wrote in the *Herald Tribune:* "Not as powerful as it should be. . . . My objection is that the play while it has its chilling and effective moments, does not make the attack on fascism as bitter and angry as it should." Atkinson in the *Times:* "Mr. Lewis has a story to tell that is calculated to make the blood of a liberal run pretty cold. . . . *It Can't Happen Here* ought to scare the daylights out of the headless American."

Howard O'Brien in the Chicago *Daily News* wrote: "I suppose one reason why I sat on the edge of my chair . . . was because I was in Germany the summer Hitler came to power. I met no German who thought that such a thing could happen there. . . . The theme of *It Can't Happen Here* is that fascism gets a hold of things because of the well-meaning people who don't recognize it for what it is."

Burns Mantle in his syndicated column, appearing in the *Chicago Tribune,* analyzed the Federal Theatre experiment: "It indicated . . . what could happen here if the social body should ever become theatre-minded in a serious way. This was a demonstration of the uses to which a people's theatre might be reasonably put. . . . Denver liked it. Boston was quite excited by it, one thousand being present and three hundred turned away. Cleveland's capacity audience shuddered a bit, but recovered and gave the actors nine curtain calls. Miami liked the play in English and Tampa was strong for the Spanish translation. Los Angeles found it pretty bold as drama and not very interesting as propaganda. Birmingham approved, Newark cheered, Bridgeport was a little stunned, San Francisco divided. Chicago took it in its critical stride, but reported audience reaction as being definitely and noisily in the play's favor."

Two productions were halted before going into rehearsal and others made local changes. New Orleans thought it unwise to produce a play about dictators in a city where Huey Long was still fresh in the minds of some people. Missouri wanted to weaken the message; Flanagan objected and the show was called off. Seattle changed the locale to the Negro section and showed how a dictatorship affects a minority group. Birmingham asked to stage it as a political rally with brass band and all; everyone was delighted to have it done that way.

When the play was moved out of the Adelphi, which displeased the stage-struck Lewis, to make way for the next scheduled play, it had played 95 performances to 110,518 people; the Yiddish version 86 to 25,160, and the Suitcase unit 133 to 179,209. With the figures of other cities, along with foreign language versions before all types of audiences, *It Can't Happen Here* played a combined total of 260 weeks, or the equivalent of a five-year run at an average Broadway house, which was a record for the time.

Flanagan's closing comments on this event were: "Not only

Federal Theatre but all people interested in possibilities of extending the boundaries of the American stage are indebted to Mr. Lewis for giving us the chance to show that a multiple production of such scope can happen here. . . . The venture was significant as an augury for the future; this was probably what President Frank Gillmore (of Actors Equity) had in mind when he wired after the production, 'Maybe the commercial managers might take a leaf out of this book and produce plays in which they have faith in different sections of the country at the same time.'

"Above all," Flanagan went on to say in her project memoir, "it was significant that hundreds of thousands of people all over America crowded in to see a play which says that when dictatorship threatens a country, it does not necessarily come by way of military invasion, that it may arrive in the form of a sudden silencing of free voices. In producing that play the first government-sponsored theatre of the United States was doing what it could to keep alive 'the free, inquiring, critical spirit' which is the center and core of democracy."

INTERMISSION

November 1936

17

PRESIDENT Roosevelt was reelected by a landslide that carried every state except Maine and Vermont. He received more votes than in 1932, showing that the American people were overwhelmingly on his side—even if the majority of newspapers were against him and the New Deal. The Depression was far from being licked, but F.D.R. had a mandate from the American people who were confident that someone in the White House was on their side.

We were still cheering the next morning when Harry Hopkins, WPA chief, turned the New Deal victory into a major defeat for WPA workers. Owing to the Midwest drought that summer, 500,000 persons were to be dropped from the payroll. Funds that Congress had voted for works projects till June 30 were to be used for the emergency. That morning Hopkins met with the four Arts directors to praise Federal One and to give them the bad news.

Flanagan considered this a betrayal of the people on the projects. They had done a good job; Hopkins had called it "phenomenal." Now the four directors would have to tell their workers that 8,000 of them would be fired as a political expedient to take care of the drought crisis.

This led Flanagan to say in *Arena:* "Art in America had hitherto been apart from politics, but these projects were at the core of life. If they were mixed with politics, it was because life in our country is mixed with politics. . . . These Arts projects were coming up, through, and out of the people. They were affected by everything affecting American life." And this mixture of life and politics was more apparent in the theatre project than in the other three projects. That is why Federal Theatre was sometimes referred to as "the show window of the WPA."

That November most activities were further complicated

by the bureaucratic changes in the local WPA administration. Federal One projects had been originally set up under General Hugh Johnson, chief of NRA; he had been succeeded by Victor Ridder as the New York City WPA administrator. Ridder was replaced in August 1936 by Colonel Brehon Somervell, who admitted that he did not believe in work relief and had less use for the Arts projects than for the construction program.

Flanagan had hoped to save New York City from layoffs. In order not to upset production plans and schedules, she had ordered cuts elsewhere and closed many small projects. But news of the impending cuts appeared in the press as rumors —rumors that were traced to Colonel Somervell's office. Arts project workers were panicky throughout the city; other WPA units joined in planning protest meetings, marches, and demonstrations. The colonel complicated the situation by announcing reprisals if they took such actions. A young Irish actor, fearing dismissal, committed suicide and intensified the need for protests.

The November ruling called for twenty percent cuts in the number of relief workers, but it did not affect the ten percent nonrelief personnel on the project. Protests soon came from various unions, including Equity and the IATSE. Washington replied that no one would be dismissed whom the Emergency Relief Bureau found was in actual need. After an investigation, the ERB reported that all reliefers were still qualified, and there was no problem about the nonrelief group.

While this arrangement was being worked out, much to the displeasure of Colonel Somervell, disorders broke out on the Arts projects. Eleven members of the militant dance unit were arrested for picketing outside the Nora Bayes Theatre off Times Square; its director, Don Oscar Becque, charged political agitation and resigned. A sitdown strike at the defunct bank building on Eight Avenue, where Hallie had her office, brought complaints from a nearby hotel. Protesters were dragged out of the building by police and fired on orders from the colonel's office.

Intermission

Afterwards some workers were reinstated and a group representing the Arts projects called on Mayor LaGuardia, who promised to take their petition to WPA officials in Washington. Then Equity forbade them from taking part in the strikes and protests, despite a petition signed by 350 members asking "Equity to bend every effort to prevent the threatened cuts in WPA relief."

On a cold January day, a mass demonstration of about 40,000 marched two abreast up Eighth Avenue. With three bands in the lead, the marchers kept moving in the crowded traffic of the avenue. It was a parade of WPA workers; their banners reminded Washington of preelection promises—not to make cuts. Instead of asking for their jobs to continue, their signs boldly read, "EXPAND WPA" to include 300,000 potential workers on home relief.

We were cheered and booed as we strode up the avenue to besiege the colonel's office in the Twelfth Regiment Armory at 70 Columbus Avenue. Arts project workers marched alongside WPA construction crews, chanting "No Cuts Today! Expand WPA! To Hell with Somervell!" Mark and I were in the parade; we yelled with the others before the fortress-like structure, while squads of mounted police sat on their horses with clubs ready—should they get orders to disperse us.

Most of the sidewalk crowd was puzzled by our protests and sitdown strikes, just as they were by those in industrial plants and factories. It struck them as odd and even silly: Uncle Sam had made jobs to put us to work. Perhaps we were boondogglers after all, they must have wondered; we did not want to work and should be tossed back on relief. They did not understand that we were not marching against work, but against insecurity. We were protesting cuts and asking for more jobs—without periodic threats of dismissals.

Many who were shocked by our tactics thought perhaps that unionization on WPA should not have been encouraged, according to Willson Whitman in a 1937 study of Federal Theatre, *Bread and Circuses.* "It may be said that the Federal Theatre administration, in accordance with the general WPA attitude, had favored the organization of workers, and for the best reasons. It must be remembered that one of the primary objects of work relief is to maintain morale.

"Early in the history of the Federal Theatre in New York, there were charges of 'un-American activities' on the project.... An inquiry conducted by Paul Blanshard, New York's Commissioner of Accounts, developed 'very little to substantiate the charges,' and it is evident that zealous patriots had once more confused union with 'un-American.' In this case the *Herald Tribune* explained that the patriots were unable to understand social workers who were considered 'to play ball with the Reds' and 'tolerate radical dogma.'"

Whitman goes on to say that trained social workers maintained that if project people were to have confidence in their abilities, they should be encouraged to organize into unions. That is why Whitman believed that some "radical dogma is tolerated, why Federal Theatre, unlike Henry Ford, refrains from chastising those who hand out CIO literature, and why the City Projects Council in New York is considered by conservatives to be a radical organization."

Federal Theatre was one of the few examples in the nation of union organization from the top down. In New York the Supervisors Council, though now functioning as a union, was set up as a mutual assistance group of producing managers to help speed up productivity and cut red tape. When the project was endangered, the group joined the fight for its continuation. There were supervisors who ignored dismissal orders until they were rescinded. It was probably the first time that such action has ever been taken by executives to protect their workers.

After the January march, Colonel Somervell joined Mayor LaGuardia on a trip to Washington to confer with WPA heads about the upheavals. Instead of presenting our demands for more jobs and no cuts, the colonel announced that no dismissals had taken place. "This is how it stands," he reported. "When I was told to make these cuts we had 10,560 people on the Arts in New York City. Now after all the trouble, the strikes, picketing and name-calling, we have 10,566."

The colonel explained that the cuts would have been made had the Arts been placed under his jurisdiction. In this struggle for complete control by the army over the liberally run projects, Hopkins was forced to intervene. Trained as a social worker and being a man with respect for the arts, Hopkins could not turn them over to the military. In order to end what *Variety* called "the contest between the army and the artists," Hopkins in mid-February removed the Arts projects from the jurisdiction of the city WPA and placed them directly under their national directors, working through Ellen Woodward, head of Federal One in Washington.

Flanagan's task was now to rebuild morale, get shows back into the shops and rehearsals, and to announce opening dates. To free herself and William Farnsworth, her Washington coordinator, for a few months of work in New York with the producing directors, she left E. C. McCleish in charge of the Washington national office. A bit later she brought Howard Miller from California to act as her administrative officer there. Before she and Farnsworth left for New York, Flanagan was assured that the present quota of 5,700 for the city would remain for six months.

Her first act in New York was to consolidate the various offices and departments under one roof to make for a more efficient working arrangement. From offices, rehearsal halls, bureaus, and other job centers she moved most of the project, except for shops, warehouses, and the information unit into the Chanin Building, a miniature skyscraper with art-deco trimmings, at Lexington and 42nd Street.

Like many structures built during the Boom, the Chanin was partly empty at the time; its owner was eager to make rental concessions to get tenants. It had housed the Republican National Committee during the 1936 election. When the project moved in, most of its furniture was still there; arrangements were made for us to take over some of it.

The first week we entered the Chanin, we were given a cool welcome by the elevator staff. Having been used to rubbing shoulders with prosperous-looking Republicans they looked us over with suspicion, snobbery, and a touch of contempt. We noticed they were mostly readers of the *Daily News* and the Hearst *Journal-American,* which always referred to WPA workers as troublemakers, radicals, reliefers, bums, and boondogglers.

My article on the Federal Theatre Circus explained why we had no elephant in the big show. Two days after the election an elephant appeared in it. Wendell Goodwin, the old-time circus press agent, jokingly announced to the press that "the pachyderm was none other than Jumbo, the star of Billy Rose's spectacle that had played the Hippodrome."

Now that the elephant's owner was a jobless professional with an animal act, he was eligible for a job on the project. The columnists in running the item gave it their own interpretation: "WPA workers (mostly Democrats) were now cracking the whip over the docile symbol of the defeated Republican party."

18

AT the Chanin, Flanagan organized the various departments into what she considered the best arrangement for the operation of the sprawling New York City project. She put William Farnsworth, a man she called an "unusual executive," in charge of administrative duties involving employment, finance, labor, and supply. She chose Philip Barber to supervise the dozen producing units; Walter Hart, production services, including a new casting bureau under Madalyn O'Shea; Kate Drain Lawson, technical department, shops and warehouses; Ted Mauntz, information and promotion; and Ed Rowland, house management and bookings.

Her job was to see that these people worked in harmony for the best interests of the project. During the first year each producing unit had its own director, designer, technicians, repertory-like company, press, and promotion. Hallie changed this so that all units could benefit from the best talents on the project. This ended the rivalries that had existed between producers and gave forgotten units a chance to shine in the Federal Theatre spectrum.

Being an early riser the tiny, energetic Flanagan got all she could out of a working day. She devoted mornings to reports from Washington and the field; to telegraphing, telephoning, or dictating letters and memos. She also dictated to her secretary in taxis while in transit from the airport, between the hotel and the office on her way to appointments for meetings and conferences. Afternoons and evenings she devoted to planning and production with directors, designers, and unit managers.

Her days were so crowded with meetings that she often only had time for a lunch of graham crackers and milk at her desk. On her free evenings the project chauffeur drove her on a round of theatres to see how our shows were doing on stage and at the box office. Afterwards she often met with directors or producers to discuss problems and future projects. She occasionally conferred with Eleanor Roosevelt to report on the progress of the project.

There was a tiny theatre atop the Chanin Building which the project used for marionette shows, a workshop to try out technical innovations, and for lectures on stage production. There were demonstrations of mobile projection and remote control switchboards. I watched Emanuel Essman, a busy project designer, display a uniform set of drafting symbols which he had devised to simplify the details of stage drawings used for multiple productions of plays.

But it was Remo Bufano's marionettes that found their perfect setting in that red-upholstered, well-appointed little theatre. As head of the project's Marionette Theatre, Bufano tried out new productions before an invited audience. I saw his dazzling show of *Old Cathay.* The figures, dressed in brilliant red, black, and gold performed before red velours; they moved, spoke, and chanted in a high-pitched, singsong voice to an oriental-sounding orchestra, composed of horns, flutes, triangles, and a large brass gong that stood at a corner of the tiny stage.

During the slowdown of activities, brought on by personnel cuts, protest demonstrations, and reorganization of the project, I contacted editors of North Carolina newspapers for whom I had once done freelance reporting and reviews, and suggested writing features, a Broadway column, and interviews with Carolinians who were "making it" in the city. In this way I got the chance to see what Broadway producers were presenting that season.

It was a time when glamorous names lit up the marquees to get audiences into theatres, regardless of the quality of the plays. Margaret Sullavan returned from Hollywood to star in a backstage formula romantic comedy, *Stage Door.* Gertrude Lawrence played Susan in *Susan and God*— a woman who had found God in a big way. Tallulah Bankhead used her husky voice to evoke life into a revival of Somerset

Intermission

Maugham's brittle comedy of marriage and divorce, *The Circle*.

I found some pleasant surprises during my reviewing stint on Broadway. Ed Wynn, one of our best comedians, clowned through an evening in *Hooray for What!* The venerable Dudley Digges gave a memorable performance in Paul Osborne's *On Borrowed Time*. Clare Boothe Luce's *The Women* had some of the smartest and most caustic dialogue heard on the stage. *Yes, My Darling Daughter* was a romantic comedy of a modern mother who had to face a more modern daughter. One of the freshest shows was *Having Wonderful Time* with a number of bright young faces.

I also saw the Abbey Players in Lennox Robinson's *The Far-Off Hills,* and the Group Theatre's stirring presentations of John Howard Lawson's *Success Story* and the Kurt Weill-Paul Green musical *Johnny Johnson.* That spring I reviewed the Theatre Union's production of *Marching Song,* the first drama with a sitdown strike. Its action was powerful, its characters were well rounded; and its set of an auto plant was designed by Howard Bay on temporary leave from the Federal Theatre. The shell of a vast, silent plant, a winter refuge for dispossessed workers and wandering derelicts, symbolized the conditions of men and machines that was as timely as the day's headlines. I was pleased that Bay, like others on the project, was beginning to have an impact on the theatre world outside our units.

After all, Hallie's dream of a "people's theatre" could only be fully realized if what we were doing had repercussions outside the project. Her vision of a theatre which was relevant to the lives of people everywhere was one that many of us shared, but which was not popular in the commercial theatre, the motion picture business, or the Congress.

We were not opposed to entertainment as some people charged, but we believed that most Americans had been taught to distrust a theatre which was "political" or which meddled with ideas that they had comfortably separated from their art and entertainment. Politics for us was not just a narrow range of human actions but central to everyone's life and thus important for the theatre to tackle.

I thought frequently of the excitement and the almost electric atmosphere on the night of the *Triple-A* premiere and believed that we had opened a door which might allow a huge breath of air to sweep through the American theatre. Here was a drama that was not only theatrical but which was charged with an urgency of current events and the necessity for understanding something critical in our lives. If the project could keep that door open, we could perhaps change the way that people viewed the theatre. Perhaps they would demand more than "satin and lumber."

In our second year we were still without open and direct opposition from Broadway show business despite an article in *Stage* that "Federal Theatre is the most important development in the power structure of the theatre since, back in the twenties, the star system and the Theatre Syndicate made theatre production a part of Big Business." Yet there were persistent rumors of troubles on the project—radicalism, cuts, extravagances—that might shut us down.

At about the time of *It Can't Happen Here,* the *Herald Tribune* headlined a story, "WPA Theatre Faces 'Revolt' of Private Groups—Producers and Unions to Start Independent Drive for Revival of Stage." When this story was checked, it had to do with picketing by members of the Musicians' Union. The men were picketing motion pictures houses—not Federal Theatre which had live orchestras in all its houses.

In the spring of 1937, the *Daily News,* speculating on the upcoming meeting of the National Theatre Council in its first convention, prophesied that it would fight the Federal Theatre and seek to replace Hallie Flanagan as its national director by an experienced Broadway producer whose outlook was that of the commercial theatre. When the group met two weeks later, it praised Flanagan for her good work and voted to consider ways of cooperating with the Federal Theatre project.

Willson Whitman, commenting on this situation in *Bread and Circuses,* wrote: "Despite efforts to stir up enmity, the legitimate theatre is not, as yet, antagonistic and does not see the Federal Theatre as a business rival. It is motion picture interests which realize that WPA productions, being low priced, are competing in their field. How could they fail to realize it when a New York critic suspected that new audiences were being recruited from neighborhood houses? When Federal Theatre directors noted that young people, at first cold to a real theatre they had never known, soon acquired a taste for it?"

The Federal Theatre's weekly national audience was a half-million, that of motion pictures was estimated at over a hundred million. It might seem that Hollywood could ignore such a small loss, but that is not the way with Big Business. That is why, from the inception of the project, the *Motion Picture Herald,* official organ of the film industry, kept a suspicious and hostile eye on the progress of the Federal Theatre.

No doubt the success of the Federal Theatre aroused the envy of some commercial producers as well as film bosses who saw success only in box office terms. We should have played down our successes, but eager as we were to show what the project could do we kept the spotlight on it. This was unwise, just as it was unwise for us to abandon the defunct bank building on the unfashionable West Side. That small, run-down building was a symbol of our status as a WPA work relief program. We lost that image when the Federal Theatre moved to the gaudy skyscraper on smart Lexington Avenue and 42nd Street.

The Chanin gave us the status of commercial success. It was a boastful and dangerous position for the project. One that made it appear more menacing, and thus more vulnerable, to all its enemies: the commercial theatre, the film industry, and the congressmen who sought to drive Uncle Sam out of show business.

19

WHILE Flanagan was busy reorganizing the New York City project at the Chanin, several changes occurred on our magazine. Since that summer when the publication had come up to Hallie's standards, she was too busy to be annoyed with de Rohan, except for his occasional sarcastic remarks about our productions in his "Box Score" column.

To his complaint that project photographers were not taking good pictures for the magazine, Flanagan allowed de Rohan to take his own and made arrangements to get a camera and other equipment for his use. Within a week he set up a dark room in a large closet and was out shooting shows. During the casting and rehearsals of *It Can't Happen Here*, he took good shots of Sinclair Lewis and the company. When the pictures appeared, he credited them to "Katz," one of his bylines to show that the magazine was no one-man operation.

But that is what it had become by winter. More and more de Rohan seemed displeased with what Portner, Mark, and I wrote. The first to quit was Portner, who grumbled about everything. De Rohan asked me to confine myself to promoting outlets to carry the magazine in the various cities where there were projects. At first I balked, as this meant "selling," which I disliked doing, but then decided it was important work and started contacting distribution centers.

Then one day de Rohan angered Mark by tossing out his article on the subject of the two groups which were benefiting most from the project—women and Negroes. They were given opportunities and recognition as project directors, held executive and supervisory posts equal to those held by men and whites. In the case of women, this was amply demonstrated with Hallie Flanagan as our national head and Ellen

Woodward as the administrative deputy of Federal One in Washington.

Mark's article called attention to the work being done by women who held important jobs in New York City: Kate Drain Lawson, technical department chief; Rosamond Gilder, recent director of the research bureau; Madalyn O'Shea, in charge of casting office; Sue Ann Wilson, director of group sales; and others in equally important posts on the project.

As to blacks, there was the Negro Theatre, along with a Negro Youth Theatre, in several cities throughout the country; they were all doing excellent work. In addition to the opportunities it gave to over a thousand actors, dancers, and singers, the project encouraged a number of black playwrights, directors, and the scenic designer Perry Watkins, who was to emerge later as a Broadway designer and producer.

De Rohan might have objected to one paragraph in Mark's story which could easily have been omitted. It concerned the USSR's policy of giving equal rights to all regardless of sex or race in the arts, industry, and government. I thought Mark had gone out of his way to glorify the Russian role in setting an example for America to follow.

"I told de Rohan to shove it," Mark told me the day he quit. "I've had it up to here."

"Tell Hallie why?"

"She's out of town. I wrote her."

"Can't you wait till she gets back?"

"I'd rather freelance."

"Will you help with *New Theatre* and the League?"

"Yes." There was a short silence, then he faced me. "I wonder how long you're going to put up with that job he gave you."

"I think distributing the magazine's a job—even if I don't like it."

"I thought you'd turn it down."

"I'm giving it a whirl for Hallie," I said. "I've gotten over a hundred outlets. Newsstands and bookshops from here to the coast. And some workers' bookshops too. The same job I did for *Contempo.*"

"I did it for mine too, but that was for the Cause."

"I believe in the Cause of Federal Theatre. And the magazine shows we haven't done a bad job for Uncle Sam."

"There's a more important job." He was again silent for a long moment. "Come to our meeting tonight. You might learn something. After all you did edit *Contempo.*"

"It was independent, Mark, with no sponsors or backers. We said and ran what we liked and belonged to no party."

"We all need discipline and direction. Without it we're wasting ammunition, getting nowhere. Meet the boys. I think you know a couple."

"Maybe I do, but I'd rather know them as I do now—with no label."

"What's wrong with that?"

I shrugged. "I'm no joiner—except the Newspaper Guild."

"Come tonight."

"Mark, I went through this at *Contempo,*" I said calmly. "When Mike Gold was in Chapel Hill, we talked about this. He's a great guy. He doesn't hide his colors. You'll never guess what he told me on the subject."

He lit a cigarette and waited for me to go on. "Mike told me not to join the Party. In fact, he said a writer was nuts to join it, and warned me to hang on to my viewpoint."

He showed no surprise, said nothing.

"Mike's no run of the mill Communist or functionary," I said. "He's tops as a man, a Party man second."

That ended our chat and dampened our friendship. I ran into Mark at different places, we were always cordial. After he left, I kept on doing promotion. De Rohan used more and more pictures and was having directors send in articles instead of reports. He went over the material and wrote what little was needed. If he aimed to drive me off, as he had Portner and Mark, he had succeeded.

I thought of writing Hallie. Then one evening I met her in the Adelphi lobby. *The Sun and I,* a play about the Pharoahs with a modern slant, had replaced the Lewis play despite its sellout engagement. She had not come to check the house or the performance but to investigate charges that Communist literature was being peddled in the lobby during intermissions. The house manager told her it had happened once or twice; now the hawker was outside and, as the sidewalk was public property, there was no way to stop him.

Satisfied that she could do nothing more about the matter, she asked me to ride down to the Maxine Elliott where Orson Welles was playing *Doctor Faustus.* We rode in the project car, driven by Hallie's favorite chauffeur, who slipped through traffic lights because the police were impressed by his big sign on the windshield, "Official Car. No. 1."

Hallie asked me how it was going at the magazine. I said that everything was all right. Then, as she knew of Mark's leaving, she questioned me about de Rohan. Instead of answering her, I asked whether she was pleased with the magazine. She nodded her approval and inquired what stories I was planning. I explained that my present job was to promote outlets for it in cities where there were Federal Theatre units.

"Very good," she said, pleased. "But that must bore you."

"Well," I nodded, "now that I've gotten over a hundred key spots to carry it."

"You mean the job's done?"

"There are other outlets but—"

"Of course," she said. "Maybe you'd like a new assignment."

"If there's one I'd—"

"There's one I think you might like," she said as the car stopped before the Maxine Elliott. "The publicity department—but not doing publicity."

"That'll be okay."

"Ted Mauntz has some writers with time on their hands. I'll ask him to let you have them as a research staff to write a history of the New York City project—back to FERA and CWA days. Would you like that?"

"Sure."

"I'll call Ted tomorrow and have him request you," she

said, stepping out of the car. "Let me know how it goes. If you don't like it, I'll find you something else."

A couple of days before I left the magazine, about fifty of us in the bureau met during our lunch hour in Kiernan and Dineen. It was a send-off party for a young Negro whose name I think was Gordon. He was quitting his job in the mailing department to join the Abraham Lincoln Brigade which was helping the Spanish Loyalists. We raised our glasses to his toast:

"I'm going over to fight those fascist bastards."

The Spanish Civil War had broken out in the summer of 1936, and the cause of the Loyalists, who represented the constitutional government of Spain, was being taken to heart by Americans of all political shades. Many of us on the project saw it as Ernest Hemingway did: a dress rehearsal of a large-scale war which Hitler and Mussolini launched in their campaign to replace democracy with worldwide fascism.

20

BY its very nature Federal Theatre, a work-relief program that aimed to perpetuate the democratic way of life, could not avoid being caught up in the mainstream of history and contributing to it. One of the critical issues of the time was the rising threat of fascism to democracy and world peace— a theme of the Sinclair Lewis play.

Fascism was a reality to most of us on the project. Mussolini's conquest of Ethiopia had ended in May of 1936 and, as if on signal, a rebellion had broken out in mid-July on the Spanish peninsula. In no time Hitler and Mussolini sent General Franco munitions, planes, and troops to back his rebel forces against the Spanish Republic.

Spain was to become a testing ground of democracy versus fascism. Its name became "evocative of imperiled democracy," writes Malcolm Goldstein in *The Political Stage.* "As both in symbol and fact, the war stirred writers to action, not only to decry the situation . . . but, for some, to make the journey to Spain and there serve as fighters or correspondents." Joining the writers were rank-and-file workers; and others included Hollywood and Broadway stars, producers, singers, actors, dancers—many of whom were on the Federal Theatre.

The cause of Spain was as much a popular front issue among liberals, radicals, and intellectuals of the Western world in the thirties as the cause of the executed anarchists, Sacco and Vanzetti, had been in the twenties. Such Americans as Hemingway, Dos Passos, and Archibald MacLeish were joined by Jean-Paul Sartre, André Malraux, Picasso, and Pablo Casals.

It was a lively time as we took sides and joined in the struggle with a fighting spirit that pushed the Depression into the background. We protested cuts and dismissals, attended rent parties, took up collections for causes close to us, cheered the steel and auto workers in their battle for union recognition, and sent bundles to the striking miners of West Virginia. With the outbreak of the Spanish rebellion, we gave parties for volunteers who went to fight and collected funds to buy medical supplies for the Loyalists.

Though most of us were strangers when we met on the projects, it was not our jobless status that brought us together as much as the causes we shared. The associations developed into a kind of comradeship best described by Malcolm Cowley, literary historian of the era: "There were certain enormous ideas working through the thirties, and one was the idea of comradeship, that you were no longer alone, isolated, helpless, but if you took the side of the working people you were one of a large body of people marching toward something."

The Spanish people epitomized what we were marching for—fairness, equality, an end to poverty as well as all other forms of slavery. We thought it unfair for the democracies to set up a Non-Intervention Policy which kept the Loyalists from getting arms, while Hitler and Mussolini were free to supply them to the Franco rebels. Knowing that it was a policy of the conservative Tory government of Stanley Baldwin and later of Neville Chamberlain, we petitioned President Roosevelt to lift the American embargo against the Loyalist defenders.

Mexico and the Soviet Union came to their rescue—with dire consequences for them. The State Department soon stopped President Cardenas, so that only the Russians sent the Loyalists arms, which were paid for in advance with Spanish gold. Spain's ports were blockaded by fascist ships; shipments ceased when much of the Soviet material failed to reach its destination. Because of Russian help, the Loyalists were branded by *Time* and the national press; in news dispatches they were called Communists and "reds," while Franco's Moorish troops and rebel forces were identified as nationalist "liberators."

Intermission

Extreme militants on the project—left-wingers and reactionaries—now had another controversial issue to bring them into open conflict. The radicals held meetings and marched, the superpatriots smeared them as "reds" in the press. Liberals joined the radicals in defending the Loyalists; Vets, Liberty Leaguers, and others were joined by Irish Catholics in backing the rebels. Members of these groups were a small minority on the project but they got in the headlines; the vast majority watched them battle each other and let the war take its course.

Volunteers from fifty countries arrived in Spain that fall to fight in the International Brigades. After two or three weeks of training they were rushed to defend Madrid from the rebels. The Loyalist government moved its capital to Valencia, leaving the people of Madrid to fight for their city. Heroine of the day was Dolores Ibarruri, *"La Pasionaria,"* whose cry, *"No Pasaran,"* stirred her countrymen to hold the city till the end of the war almost three years later.

The winter of 1936, Hemingway was sent by the North American Newspaper Alliance (NANA) to cover the war from the the Loyalist side, a job that was being well done by Herbert L. Matthews of the *New York Times.* Hemingway was also involved with *Spain in Flames,* a film put together from film news clips, for which he had written a statement that the Spanish people were fighting absentee landlords, Moors, Italians, and Germans. Thirty-seven years old at the time and working on *To Have and Have Not,* Hemingway saw the Spanish struggle as "a dress rehearsal for the inevitable European conflict." He was serving NANA as "an anti-war correspondent," according to Carlos Baker, his biographer, to keep the United States from being drawn into the future war.

In February, Hemingway and a group of Spanish sympathizers, including Dos Passos, MacLeish, and Lillian Hellman started making *The Spanish Earth,* a documentary film to show the plight of the Spanish people. While Dos Passos aimed to present the suffering of the people, Hemingway was more interested in the military aspect of their struggle.

Much of the film was shot under fire in and around Madrid, the first European city bombed by blitz warfare. Hemingway was often with Herbert Matthews and their sympathetic reports raised our hopes that the embargo might be lifted.

When Hemingway finished *The Spanish Earth,* he flew to New York to present the Loyalist cause before the Writers Congress of the League of American Writers. Carnegie Hall was packed, and I was one among the thousands who were turned away. Lawrence Gellert, whose Negro folk music had been used in Tamiris's *How Long Brethren?* described it to me as an unforgettable event; he said, among other things, that Hemingway proved to be a more effective writer than a speaker. The June heat forced the impassioned Hemingway, who was too warmly dressed for the occasion, to claw at his tie and collar while he spoke under the glaring lights.

Hemingway was introduced by MacLeish, who later quit his editorial post on *Fortune* partly because of Henry Luce's consistent anti-Loyalist policy in *Time* and *Life.* In his seven-minute speech Hemingway said, "A writer's problem does not change as he himself changes, but his problem remains the same. It is to write truly and, having found what is truth, to project it in such a way that it becomes part of the experience of the person who reads it. Really good writers are always rewarded under any system of government that they can tolerate. There is only one government that cannot produce writers and that is the system of fascism. For fascism is a lie told by bullies. A writer who cannot lie cannot live and work under fascism."

The crowd cheered Hemingway with a standing ovation. After all, he was then America's top writer. Known as a non-political figure, Hemingway gave the Loyalist supporters respectability among those Americans who called them "reds"; and their cause, according to Professor Baker, seemed to have awakened the writer's social consciousness.

The Spanish Earth was shown at that meeting by Joris Iven, the Dutch film maker who was its technical director. Though a narration had been recorded for it by Orson Welles, who was busy at the time on Blitzstein's *The Cradle*

Intermission

Will Rock, Hemingway was persuaded to write and record his own. The film had as yet no music track according to Virgil Thomson, who recently told me about it. He and Blitzstein assembled one from recordings owned by Gerald Murphy and Paul Bowles; choral numbers sung by miners and peasants, woodwind *coblas* of Barcelona; and flamenco, which Thomson said they used to underscore the fascists.

In July, Martha Gellhorn, the writer-journalist who was to become Hemingway's third wife, arranged through her friend Eleanor Roosevelt for Hemingway to show the film at the White House before the President, Harry Hopkins, and others. Hemingway hoped that it would persuade F.D.R. to ask Congress to lift the arms embargo. Nothing came of it; there was too much pressure from British Tories, the Roman Catholic church, superpatriots, and conservative congressmen.

That summer Hemingway also showed the film before a group of Hollywood stars assembled by Frederic March and his wife Florence Eldridge. Hemingway made a short speech, asking for funds to help the Loyalists get ambulances and medical supplies. Also present was Scott Fitzgerald, who admired his friend's efforts for Spain. Fitzgerald described Hemingway as keyed up to the point of "nervous tensity." He heard Hemingway say that "the big fight was fascism," and watched him breeze around Hollywood "like a whirlwind," in his efforts to help the Loyalists. Hemingway was to write his only play, *The Fifth Column,* and his most popular novel, *For Whom the Bells Toll,* about the Spanish War.

A Spanish Fiesta was staged that fall in fashionable Washington Mews on lower Fifth Avenue. The cobblestoned one-block street was lined on both sides with tents, booths, floats, and platforms for musicians, speakers, and flamenco dancers. With Donald Ogden Stewart as Master of Ceremony, Gypsy Rose Lee stripped for Spain, Tamiris danced, Tallulah Bankhead charmed everyone with her husky laugh, and a big sheep dog was raffled off for the price of an ambulance. I was dressed as a swami in a booth, reading palms of celebrities who contributed to the purchase of a medical unit, which was being organized by Dr. Edward E. Barsky. Also attending was Helen Hayes, head of the Spanish children's milk fund; members of her committee included Brooks Atkinson and Clifford Odets.

Months later Arts project workers and sympathizers in a darker mood crowded into Carnegie Hall to attend memorial services for Americans who had died on Spanish soil as members of the Abraham Lincoln and George Washington battalions fighting with the international brigades. While honoring them, appeals were made for funds to buy ambulances and medical supplies for the Loyalists in their single-handed fight against the newly formed Rome-Berlin-Tokyo axis.

On April 26, 1937, the world was shocked by the most savage and deliberate bombardment of the Spanish war. On that day the Nazi air command experimented with the effects of a systematic and completely destructive attack on a defenseless open town. "The town was Guernica, sacred to the Basques as their medieval capital," wrote Matthews in his remarkable memoir of the war, *Half of Spain Died.* "The bombing was a huge success, but it will live forever in infamy. Out of one man's anger came what many believe to be the greatest painting of the century, Picasso's GUERNICA."

ACT THREE

The Show Goes On
1937-1938

21

Here is the challenge to our democracy.
... I see one-third of a nation ill-housed,
ill-clad, ill-nourished. It is not in despair that I paint you that picture. I
paint it too you in hope—because the
nation, seeing and understanding the
injustice of it—proposes to paint it out.

—Franklin D. Roosevelt, 2nd Inaugural
Address.

I had moved over to the press department of the project and
was working with a staff of writers on its early history when
F.D.R. was inaugurated for a second term. Along with Hallie
Flanagan we asked ourselves: What part could a government-
supported theatre take in helping to realize his words—despite cuts, dismissals, protests, and the conservative stand
that the Federal Theatre should not present economic issues?

"It was logical that a theatre which had its roots in economic need should be concerned in some of its plays with
economic conditions," Flanagan said in *Arena*. "Federal
Theatre should not restrict itself to drama on social themes,
should not overemphasize such themes, and should keep
steadily in mind that plays were to be chosen for their value
as plays. Yet it was strikingly true that our playwrights and
playgoers cared about economic and social plays."

The nationwide reception of *It Can't Happen Here, Triple-
A Plowed Under, Class of '29, Chalk Dust, Battle Hymn,* and
Altars of Steel, which had recently opened in Atlanta, proved
to all of us that audiences wanted them. These plays presented the struggle of people trying to grasp the social forces
at work and to achieve through them a better life for more

people. Thousands of people in the nation must have considered such themes dramatic—to buy tickets weeks in advance of opening dates.

When the Living Newspaper's *Power* opened in February 1937, sixty thousand tickets had been sold before the curtain rose. The critics were unanimous in praise of the show, though some were disturbed by its theme of educating the consumer about utilities.

When Harry Hopkins saw *Power,* he told Flanagan and the large cast backstage, "This is a great show. I want this play and plays like it done from one end of the country to the other. You will take a lot of criticism on this play. People will say it's propaganda. Well, I say, what of it? It's propaganda to educate the consumer who's paying for power. It's about time someone had some propaganda for him. The power companies have spent millions on propaganda for the utilities. It's about time that the consumer had a mouthpiece. I say more plays like *Power* and more power to you."

After he left the Biltmore with Flanagan, Hopkins said, "Well, I guess I stuck my neck out."

"You're certainly on the record," she reports in her memoir, "and I take it that you think we're on the right track."

That evening they dined with Langdon Post, now Tenement House Commissioner for New York City; and the trio started to plan a Living Newspaper on housing, which was to open a year later as *One-Third of a Nation.* The subject was close to Hopkins who, from the inception of the project, had asked Flanagan to do something about the intolerable tenements in Chicago. Its own Living Newspaper's *Model Tenement* had been banned by the Mayor of Chicago in the early months of the project.

Power was one of the two big successes which opened during the winter upheaval of cuts, protest demonstrations, and Colonel Somervell's attempted military takeover of the Arts. The other was *The Tragical History of Doctor Faustus* by Christopher Marlowe. It was produced by Houseman and directed by Welles, who also played the title role. Jack Carter, star of their Harlem *Macbeth,* portrayed the cunning Mephistopheles.

Act Three

Doctor Faustus was an artistic hit as well as a first-rate magic show. The Maxine Elliott stage was in total darkness except for the artful use of spots. Trapdoors opened and closed swallowing up actors, props, and stagehands in explosions of yellowish smoke. With claps of thunder and streaks of lightning Faustus rose from the blackness on a platform that projected into the audience. Puppets of the Seven Deadly Sins played at his feet, deformed and slithering in their lewdness. Mephisto, calm and amused, rarely raised his voice as he drew Faustus into his midnight seances. Helen, the big prize, turned out to be a masked apparition.

The critics reported that the Marlowe play had never been staged with such magic—magic being the point of that drama as well as the invisible ingredient of all good theatre. They agreed that Welles and his company, including Bil and Cora Baird, who created the puppets, evoked "the musical majesty of Marlowe"; and the production was showered with such adjectives as "daring, striking, original, startling."

The only dissenting voice was that of the project's staunchest friend, Burns Mantle of the *Daily News.* He wrote in a newspaper whose editorial policy opposed such plays he was recommending: "It seems to me that the people's theatre would be better employed, considering the greatest good for the greatest number, in producing plays of timely significance."

Though directors were encouraged to do such plays, we believed that a people's theatre should also produce classics. Our audiences seemed to agree and flocked to see the show. *Doctor Faustus,* scheduled for a limited engagement, had a six-month sellout run. When Mantle heard of its success, he wrote that it was a tribute to the Federal Theatre's revival of the classic.

Yet Mantle, like most newspapermen, had the last word: "It does not follow that a modern play of social import would not have drawn equally well . . . achieved far more in electrifying and stimulating a puzzled people's thought. . . . We are passing through times of social stress, of which WPA is an expression. . . . More serious devotion should be centered on the problems of the people it seeks to serve."

Uncle Sam Presents

With such words from one of the nation's outstanding critics and Hopkins' enthusiasm for *Power,* the project was encouraged to plan more social dramas for that spring, 1937. First to open in May was the Jewish Theatre unit's *Professor Mamlock* by Friedric Wolf, an exiled German writer. The play concerned the persecution of a German surgeon who could not grasp the political changes which occurred in the early thirties. The rise of Hitler ruined him completely, sending him home, beaten and stunned, with a sign around his neck, "JEW."

During the early run of the drama, a real Professor Mamlock, an exiled German doctor, arrived in New York seeking refuge from the Nazis who had ruined his life and left him penniless. He had been at the head of the dental department of the University of Berlin. Many details of his life and career, including the fact that he had received the Iron Cross for bravery in the war, were like those of the professor in our play.

Critics and columnists devoted much space to the play. Ernest L. Meyer wrote in the *Post,* "I recommend *Professor Mamlock* for one thing: its dramatic unfolding of the fact that it can happen anywhere." He went on to speak about lynchings in the South and and labor discrimination in the North, concluding, "Until we check the vicious and illegal use of force against racial, religious, and political minorities, we shall face the same disaster that faced Professor Mamlock, who did not smell until it was too late the brimstone of hatred in the air of his once free country."

The democratic principle of racial equality was dramatized in the spirit of modern dance by Tamiris, one of the project's most inventive choreographers. Her production of *How Long Brethren?* proved so popular on Broadway that Flanagan invited Tamiris and the company to give performances at the Federal Theatre summer session at Vassar. It was a spirited presentation of authentic folk material from Lawrence Gellert's collection of *Negro Songs of Protest.*

To the singing of a Negro chorus, led by Eva Jessye of *Porgy and Bess* fame, Tamiris and her group danced seven episodes of Negro life, all simple in form but dramatic in their intensity. Jerome Bohm, dance critic of the *Herald Tribune* wrote: "In *How Long Brethren?* Tamiris has accomplished the finest composition of her career. The most thrilling episode, 'Let's Go to the Buryin',' with its frenzied emotional climax heightened by Tamiris's superb dancing, aroused the audience to a state of high excitement." The production won the *Dance Magazine* Award for the best choreography of the year.

It was a thrilling performance made more so by the fact that I had gotten to know Tamiris while researching the dance article for the magazine. And it was further testimony to the creative resources of the project. I hoped as I watched Tamiris that evening that I would be able to do Flanagan and the entire New York unit justice in the history that Hallie had assigned me to write.

22

EARLY in February 1937, I reported to the information department to begin work on the history of the project. During my year on the magazine I had learned a great deal about the operation of the Federal Theatre and had made some close friends. But three writers had already left our staff because of de Rohan's silent campaign to take complete control of the publication and I, too, felt that my welcome was worn out. Though I did not look upon my new assignment with eager anticipation, I was as happy to leave the magazine as I was to see Roosevelt in the White House for another four years.

After meeting Ted Mauntz, a slight, energetic ex-newspaperman, who was head of the information office, I was introduced to Harry Davis, a soft-voiced and friendly person who was to act as my supervisor. A freelance writer, he had the respect of the dozen or more press agents and newsmen on his staff, whose stories and features he had to clear before they were released to the press. He was to serve me in a similar capacity, assigning writers, furnishing material, and checking on the progress of the project.

Davis gave me a small office away from the press department. It had bare walls, two desks and typewriters, a long table and chairs, but no telephone. The office was near the elevators and the spot where we signed the time sheet in the morning. The remainder of the day we were on our own, to work in the office or out "in the field," as we indicated on the sheet, to do research in the library or to interview directors and heads of the various units.

On the long table Davis placed two huge black, overstuffed scrapbooks of clippings covering the activities of the project: one was dated 1933–35, the other 1935–36. Davis said they were to serve as basic material for the pre-WPA and WPA history; they could be supplemented by research in the theatre section of the public library at Fifth Avenue and 42nd Street. I suggested that we also use the file of *Federal Theatre Magazine,* statements which Flanagan had made to national and regional directors, and articles she had written for such publications as *Theatre Arts Monthly.*

"Fine," he said. "Do you have this material?"

"Some. I'll bring it tomorrow."

"Let me know what you don't have. I'll try and get it for you. Have an idea when you want the boys to start?"

"In a couple of days," I replied, looking over the scrapbooks. "I'll work up a preliminary outline for you."

"The sooner the better. And tell me how many you'll need to research and help write it," Davis said. "You can have three or four right off. But how long you can keep them will depend on our upcoming spring and summer shows."

I spent the first day checking the older scrapbook. Most of it covered the activities of the Civil Works Administration (CWA) and the Temporary Emergency Relief Administration (TERA) of the city and state. In 1935 the program was taken over and expanded by the Roosevelt administration into the new alphabetical FERA, PWA and finally the WPA, headed by Harry Hopkins, which included the four Arts projects.

During the early days of the city and state project, theatrical troupes of unemployed actors, some from relief rolls and others through Actors Equity and various theatrical unions, furnished free entertainment to children and older people in parks, schools, and settlement houses. At first only a few hundred were employed, putting on plays, musicals, vaudeville, and puppet shows. Two of the most popular groups were the circus and the Gilbert and Sullivan companies playing the five boroughs.

Reading the yellowed clippings, I saw evidence of what Mark had told me: most relief projects were set up as a result of continuous agitation by activists, chiefly left-wingers and the unemployed, who had marched on City Hall and demanded jobs instead of demoralizing home relief. These protest demonstrations had frightened politicians and bankers into thinking there might be a revolution if something were not done soon to relieve the suffering brought on by bank failures, the Depression, and the do-nothing Hoover administration.

I now moved down to Chelsea, but I could still walk to work. That day I took my folder of notes home to prepare a rough outline from what I had read. Before retiring around midnight, I strolled along 23rd Street; it was chilly, a sharp wind blew from the Hudson. I stopped in front of the balconied structure of the Chelsea Hotel, then home of two young writers whose early novels I liked: Thomas Wolfe and James T. Farrell. I remembered Fitzgerald's reluctance about the project and his advice about writing and I determined to give Hallie a history that would please her.

The following morning I typed an outline of some twenty chapters that made up the first section of the history. I left it with Davis who was surprised to have it so soon. Without the knowledge I had picked up on the magazine, I could not have done it in such a short time. A bit later Davis told me Mauntz approved and asked him to assign me writers to work on it. Before the day was over I met four writers, discussed the nature of our history, and gave them research assignments.

The first writer I saw was James Hughes, well-dressed, prematurely gray, and in his early forties; his pince-nez gave him a distinguished look. The only one of the group who had worked in the commercial theatre, Jim had graduated from Columbia and was a close friend of Richard Watts, critic of the *Herald Tribune.* I was pleased Hughes decided to research and write the opening chapter on the desperate state of the Broadway theatre, which had been caused by the combined effects of radio, movies, and the Depression.

Max Shohet was a newspaperman who knew more about the politics of the period than of the theatre until he joined the press department. He was small of stature, alert, and always sported a pipe. Having flirted with Marxism, he had definite opinions and stood up to the proselytizing radicals on and off the project. His work had been with the Children's

Act Three

Theatre whose production of *The Emperor's New Clothes* had been playing for almost a year. Because of this background I assigned Shohet the chapter on the program of the Children's Theatre.

Jack Seligman was a tall, frail, pock-faced young man who had been in and out of hospitals with lung problems. He was a freelance writer with a wife and baby and was having a difficult time making ends meet on his $23.86 weekly salary. For all his personal problems, he was energetic and had done well with the Suitcase Theatre and the Gilbert and Sullivan units, which he publicized from time to time.

I cannot remember the name of the fourth writer Davis sent me that day. He was short, studious, and carelessly dressed, and had a mysterious air about him. He hoped to be a playwright and spoke of his interest in a novelty of the time: psychodrama, an early form of group therapy in which troubled individuals worked out their neuroses on a small stage. I never learned what he had done in the press department, but he accepted the assignment to research the chapter on our foreign-language units—German, Yiddish, and Anglo-Jewish.

While they were researching in the files of the press department or at the library, I expanded my piece on the circus with the assistance of Wendell Goodwin, the heavy-set, jovial Irishman who had belonged to the Big Top. Goodwin was too busy with the circus or I would have asked him to write the article from the viewpoint of someone who knew the circus —its animals, clowns, acrobats, and stunt performers—from personal experiences.

Within a week the writers brought me pages of notes and parts of chapters they had begun to write. I went over them, made notations in the margin, and showed them to Davis. He had minor suggestions which I added to mine, and I then discussed them with the writers in my small office, at lunch, or during coffee breaks in the cafeteria on the ground floor of the building. After writing the circus chapter, I went over material for a chapter on the multiple productions of *It Can't Happen Here.*

The history file was taking shape when the inevitable happened. One morning Davis walked into my office and said that Hughes had been transferred to James Bridie's *Tobias and the Angel.* That afternoon he sent me Hughes' replacement, a young writer who showed no interest in the historical chapter. I decided to finish it and gave him a new assignment—a chapter on the Negro Theatre and its work in the Harlem community. That same week I lost Shohet, but was fortunate in turning over his Children's Theatre material to a bright college graduate with writing experience.

With spring and summer plans in the news, I suspected that the history project was doomed. One by one my original staff was assigned to upcoming shows. Within a month I was left only with replacements. Finally, I realized that the history was started during a lull in the department to keep its writers temporarily busy while on the payroll.

When I was the last one on the history, I spoke to Flanagan and explained the situation. Though she understood what was happening, she was disappointed that the work would have to be delayed or temporarily set aside, but hoped that I might continue doing what I could to keep it alive. I promsied her I would—even if it meant my working on it with no other writer in the press department.

I was a one-man staff for a very short time. Mauntz called to tell me that he was losing one of his best press agents to the Warner Bros. press department: Allan Meltzer, who had publicized the Welles-Houseman Harlem *Macbeth, Horse Eats Hat,* and *Doctor Faustus,* which was still playing at the Maxine Elliott.

"I'd like you to replace Allan," Mauntz said.

"What about our history?" I asked, surprised. "Hallie's all for it."

"It'll have to wait," he said. "Let's have all your stuff. We might get back to it—when there's another lull."

There was never again such a lull.

23

THE Federal Theatre information department occupied most of the floor in the big office-factory building at 71 West 23rd Street at the corner of Sixth Avenue. To the east were the Flatiron Building and Madison Square Park; to the west, an Automat and a friendly bar which became a staff hangout, and the stately Chelsea Hotel. That office was the only place where I had to sign a time sheet; if we showed up a few minutes after nine we were docked an hour.

There were about one hundred and fifty on the staff; it was divided into about ten units, each with its own supervisor, all under Ted Mauntz. The units were publicity, scholastic press, promotion and group sales, poster and program printing, sign shop, radio division and photographic. All were on that floor except the sign and print shop, radio and photographic. Harry Davis briefed me on the overall department and its supervisors. He was a writer with a literary background; he knew *Contempo* and seemed glad to have me on his regular staff.

Since Federal Theatre was restricted to advertising its shows in Monday "abc" columns, our task as press agents was to grab all the space we could on or off the drama pages. We prepared stories and features, planted column items and gags, arranged promotional tie-ins and stunts, and suggested ideas for interviews to the city desks. We also had to prepare a press book on the show, set up photographs for principals, rehearsal and production shots, caption pictures, and prepare material for drama editors. Then we had to get together copy for houseboards, signs, posters, programs, all with official billing, and to supply information for use by radio unit, scholastic press, foreign press, and group sales.

Group sales and scholastic press arranged for theatre parties to attend our shows. Frank Goodman, youthful head of the scholastic department, circularized schools and college publications with news of our productions. It was a job that was close to Flanagan's heart—introducing young people to live theatre. Hallie Jonas supervised the group sales unit; her staff sold blocks of tickets to social organizations to build up an advance before the shows opened. They worked with schools, hospitals, trade unions, and charitable groups raising funds for a variety of causes.

We also had units housed at 1697 Broadway, which was to become project headquarters and Flanagan's office after a thirty percent personnel cut later that year. Richard Rose headed a staff of a dozen cameramen; he assigned photographers to take pictures of principals, rehearsal, and scene shots. One of his best men was Arthur Steiner, whose glamorous-looking photographs of Ardis Gaines for Bernard Shaw's *On the Rocks* got her to Hollywood, where she became Brenda Marshall.

The radio division, with Evan Roberts as director and Ivan Black as press agent, produced the weekly Federal Theatre of the Air, in addition to shows promoting current project attractions. At the time the unit was presenting a Repertory of the Air with plays by Molière, Ibsen, Goldoni, Goldsmith, and Chekhov. The plays were directed by Howard da Silva, who had worked with the Cleveland project, and prior to that with Eva LeGallienne's Civic Repertory.

We were sometimes entertained by two members of the press department, Wendell Goodwin of the circus and Bill Bentley, a fun-loving Irishman, who did odd jobs along with conning shopkeepers to let him place our show posters in their display windows. Goodwin dressed like a roustabout, talked and smelled like one; Bentley was full of yarns. He always had an adventure locating spots for our posters; after a luckless day, he would announce with a long face, "This is one of my the-lady-said-no-days."

Billing, a chronic ailment of the entertainment world, meant a trip uptown to double-check copy on houseboards, posters, and signs to make sure the spelling and type sizes of names of actors, authors, and production staff were correct. Sometimes we did not discover an error until it was too late. A glaring one I missed was on *The Cradle Will Rock* house-board at the Maxine Elliott: "Light*n*ing by Feder." There was a complaint from Abe who, having lit Welles' shows, considered himself a star.

The early spring day I reported to Houseman, he and Welles were preparing Marc Blitzstein's *The Cradle Will Rock*. The Maxine Elliott, with its yellowing marble and faded brocades, still showed traces of its glamorous days when Ethel Barrymore, Jeanne Eagles, and Jane Cowl had starred there. Houseman's office was in the basement, which was the lounge leading to the ladies' powder room. Its carpet was worn and the walls were a washed-out pink. At the foot of the stairs sat Augusta Weissberger, his plump, light-hearted secretary who had been with the pair since their *Macbeth* days in Harlem.

Houseman sat at a nearby desk. He was that rare man in the theatre, calm, urbane, and intelligent who spoke with a slight British accent which created the impression that he ran an endowed college rather our most imaginative pro-ducing unit. Knowing what he wanted, Houseman asked me to prepare a pressbook on the show and not send out a line without clearing it with him. He set up policy for the show; I followed through and we never had an unfriendly word.

He took me upstairs to meet Orson Welles in a semidark backstage dressing room. We found Welles dozing fully dressed on a shabby chaise lounge, his face to the wall. Houseman called his name, saying that he wanted him to meet their new press agent. The bulky twenty-two-year-old "boy wonder of the theatre" aroused himself and turned a bloated baby face toward me. With his small, sluggish eyes, and flanking the stub of a nose which was like that of a statue with a missing part, he squinted as though coming out of a fog. Then he grunted, turned away, his bulky mass rolled over, and he went back to sleep.

"Orson rehearses at the oddest hours," Houseman said by

way of apologizing for him. "Sometimes he starts at midnight and works with the principals till dawn. I want you to meet Marc Blitzstein. He's the star of *Cradle.* Come see him tomorrow."

Marc Biltzstein was a swarthy, smallish man in his early thirties, with a dark moustache that emphasized his gypsy-like features. I found him friendly, quick, articulate, and, like Houseman, to the point. He was dedicated to the Federal Theatre, as he was to the cause of the Spanish Loyalists and the American Labor Movement, not for political reasons but because of his sense of justice. His father was a Philadelphia banker and an old-line Socialist, advanced in ideas, conservative in his musical tastes. Blitzstein said that his own political conversion happened during the Depression and the early days of the New Deal.

Blitzstein went to Europe to study with Schoenberg and the legendary Nadia Boulanger, who considered him a brilliant young composer. Later, while summering at Provincetown, he wrote a skit around a streetwalker's song, "Nickle Under the Foot." His idols at the time were Bertolt Brecht and Kurt Weill, whose *Threepenny Opera* had deeply impressed him as a modern stage musical work. Brecht was in New York at the time; Blitzstein sought him out to show him his song.

"Brecht liked it," Blitzstein told me when I interviewed him that week. "The melody pleased him. Its jazz or blues spirit. But my lyric wasn't acid enough. He wanted it to have more bite. More the savage quality of his lyrics for *Threepenny Opera.* When I told him my ambition was to write an American *Threepenny,* he said, if I was serious, I must make prostitution a dramatic symbol for overall prostitution—contemporary man's sellout of his talent, his soul, and dignity to the powers that exploit mankind."

Blitzstein went to work and wrote *Cradle* in less than two months of inspired composing and dedicated it to Brecht. Then came the job of auditioning. He played the piano score and sang its songs for such serious Broadway producers as Herman Shumlin, Harold Clurman, Charles Friedman, and members of the Actors Repertory Company which had re-

Act Three

cently done *Let Freedom Ring.* The latter promptly accepted it for production in its 1936–37 season.

"The Actors' Rep was broke, they had to drop it," Blitzstein told me. "I made the rounds once more. Orson Welles, who was to have directed it for the Rep, now spoke of finding a producer for it. Nothing came of it until he got me together with John Houseman who was sharing an apartment with Virgil Thomson. Houseman was impressed and wanted to produce it although Virgil, who was suspicious of radical ideas, wanted me to stick to serious composition.

"I wasn't surprised that Houseman wanted *Cradle.* He'd already produced Archibald MacLeish's *Panic* which was certainly progressive and which had played for mostly young left-wingers at the Phoenix. But Welles surprised me. Until then he had done nothing but arty classics. I may have been responsible for making him politically conscious with *Cradle*—or, perhaps, it was the Spanish Loyalists, or the temper of the times, because Orson is too much of a showman not to be in tune with them.

"While *Panic* said something about bank failures, the Depression, and the collapse of capitalism during the Hoover years of breadlines and balanced budgets, *Cradle* goes a step beyond it. Some say it's proletarian, but I say it's middle-class. Ordinary workers and average Americans being swallowed up by big business and industry. My 'stormbirds' sound like they're bringing the revolution, but they're really bringing a warning of the threat posed by home-grown dictators, political or industrial, and such fascist front groups as the Liberty League. We have to be on our guard before they get a stranglehold on America."

During that interview Blitzstein said that it was Houseman who arranged for Flanagan to come for dinner to their apartment in late March 1937, and then to hear him play and sing the *Cradle* score. He could tell that she was sold on it from the first song. She was carried away by the hypnotic intensity that was to characterize performances of the work later. For Flanagan saw *Cradle* as her kind of theatre. It had an agitprop vitality. She had to have it for the project.

133

Uncle Sam Presents

"It took no wizardry to see that . . . this was something new," Flanagan wrote in *Arena*. "This was in its percussive as well as its verbal beat Steel Town U.S.A.—America, 1937. Jack Houseman would produce it, and Orson Welles would direct it, and I didn't see why they needed any scenery. Orson, however, wanted illuminated wagons, and while they were being fought over, I forgot about *The Cradle* in the thunder and lightning surrounding the project itself."

The year 1937 was in many ways the most chaotic and troubled of the Depression. Though the New Deal had been vindicated by the election, there were, despite spurts of recovery and recession, conservative cries of cutting relief spending. All such attempts were met by strikes and demonstrations by WPA workers throughout the country. Added to this was the agitation and drive by industrial workers fighting for their rights under the new Wagner Act to organize into unions and bargain collectively with big business. It was a year of labor and industrial violence in auto factories and steel mills, and of fascist advances on the international and home fronts.

"There was some feeling later, in New York and Washington, that Hallie had been irresponsible in allowing so controversial a piece to be presented at such a precarious time," Houseman records in his memoir. "I believe she knew exactly what she was doing. She had no way of guessing . . . that a double accident of timing would project us all onto the front pages of the nation's press; but she did sense which way the political winds were blowing and realized, better than her more timid colleagues, that in the storm into which the Arts projects were headed, there was no safety in prudence and no virtue in caution."

24

F.D.R.! F.D.R.!

Don't Deceive Us!
We Believed You!
Don't Juggle WPA!

Have you forgotten your promise to
relief workers and the unemployed?

Have you surrendered to the Chamber
of Commerce, Hearst, and the whole
reactionary Wall Street Gang whose
"Starve America" program you once
promised to fight tooth and nail?

Protect Your Job!
Join the Workers' Alliance Today!

THREATS of wholesale dismissals and rumors that the project might fold in June 1937, seemed to keep pace with the rising strife on the industrial front. While John L. Lewis, organizer of the miners, pushed his drive to unionize steel workers into the CIO, a militant offshoot of the conservative AFL, relief workers marched, picketed, passed out leaflets, and raised their voices for the continuation and expansion of the projects.

MAYOR LA GUARDIA!

In Washington you said, "WPA must be
continued and enlarged. In New Orleans,
you said, "Relief in New York is too low."

SATURDAY APRIL 4, 1937
!!March!!
(from Battery Park 11 A.M.)

135

Uncle Sam Presents

On to City Hall
MARCH TO MAKE THE MAYOR ACT!

Then came May Day. A memorial parade of 30,000 over-flowing into Union Square, marching, singing slogans, carry-ing banners, showering the streets with leaflets. Banners of vivid colors waving in the wind. The Federal Theatre, Dance Unit, the Art, Music, and Writers projects. WPA construction crews in overalls.

We were chanting and carrying banners. No WPA cuts! More jobs! Garment workers supporting miners, steel and auto workers fighting for union recognition under the Wag-ner Act. Red and yellow banners—Hitler and Mussolini: "Take Your Dirty Hands Off Spain!" Red and gold Chinese banners—Japan: "Get Out of China!" Red, white, and blue banners—F.D.R.: "Lift the Arms Embargo!"

In this highly charged and strife-torn atmosphere, inside and outside Federal Theatre, *The Cradle Will Rock* re-hearsed at the Maxine Elliott. While *Faustus* nightly put on its magic show of thunder and lightning, *Cradle* was like a time bomb waiting to explode in the rising industrial war-fare and the turmoil on the project. At one end of the stage Orson Welles coached actors in their roles; at the piano, Blitzstein rehearsed others with their songs, while Lehman Engel, the conductor borrowed from the music project, stood by. I waited between the *Faustus* black velours for my cue to interview the principals for press material.

With the exception of Will Geer, a popular actor and singer at scores of union picnics and hillbilly song fests, the large cast was from the project. Geer was brought in to play Mr. Mister, the dictator-boss of Steeltown. The role of Larry, the foreman, was being played by Howard da Silva, who had been discovered on the radio project by Welles. I heard his voice for the first time when he rehearsed with Blitzstein:

> One big question inside me cries
> How many frame-ups,
> How many shake-downs,

May Day Parade, 1937

Uncle Sam Presents

How many sell-outs
How many toiling, ailing,
Dying, piled-up bodies,
Brother,
Does it take to make you wise?

When I got my chance to talk with the rangy, middle-westerner with the twangy voice, Geer told me he loved to play mean roles like the boss in *Cradle*, and the racist in *Let Freedom Ring* even though he had once been the victim of a gang of pro-Nazi thugs. While he was out in Hollywood, where he organized the West chapter of the Group Theatre, and was directing a production of Odets' *Till the Day I Die*, he was kidnapped by members of the Friends of Germany and so badly beaten that he had to be hospitalized.

"In *Let Freedom Ring*, I played Pap, the best drawn character in this play," Geer told me as he stretched out his long legs. "A backwoods critter of tough pioneer stock—and a racist. I'm reminded by one of the characters that Negroes have rights too. When I auditioned for the part for Albert Bein, the author and producer, I showed up at his office with my guitar and said, 'I hear you're doing an uprising play. I like uprising plays. I'll sing you an uprising song I made up myself!'"

The role was perfect for him, for Pap was a ballad-singing man who played a wire-strung fiddle, and Geer could play that too. He got the part and did a lot to make the drama a success. Geer said he loved to play preachers too—good and bad ones. In Paul Green's *Unto Such Glory*, his Brother Simpkins was a wily revivalist who tried to seduce the wife of a young mountaineer. But it was a folksy sort of play, with down-to-earth humor, and no political message. He did the play for the One-Act Experimental Company during a previous short stint on the project.

While Geer stemmed mostly from the political and social theatre, Howard da Silva's background was in classics. A native of Cleveland, he came to New York and was an apprentice at Eva Le Gallienne's Civil Repertory at nineteen, appearing in revivals of Shakespeare, Ibsen, Chekhov, and Goldoni. From there he went to the Cleveland Playhouse, where he played leading roles in classic and modern plays. Then back to New York; though da Silva was never a Group Theatre actor, he did appear in the first *Waiting for Lefty* and later in *Golden Boy.*

This led to his landing a job on the Federal Theatre radio project, where he was engaged to direct a series of plays. The first series was called "Labor on the March," a history of the labor movement; then "The Great Drama" series of plays he had done at the Civic Repertory. Asked how he had come to the attention of Orson Welles, who took him on as a nonrelief actor for *Cradle,* da Silva said that it was because of his radio work.

"Almost everyday I'd run into Orson at one of the radio studios," da Silva told me at the time. "He was playing 'The Shadow' and doing voices on the *March of Time.* I knew him but he didn't know me. He was always on the run—coming or going. I knew he was playing in *Horse Eats Hat* and *Faustus.* Taxis waited for him in front of the studios—so he could make his curtain. One day he stopped me and asked if I'd like to be in a show of his. He told me it was *Cradle.* He'd heard my voice. It was loud and big. Just what he wanted for Larry. So here I am."

The other principals were played by Peggy Coudray, Hiram Sherman, Olive Stanton, and Paula Lawrence, who had been in *Horse Eats Hat* and was currently playing the masked Helen in *Faustus.* Peggy Coudray had been a Broadway soubrette in musicals and operettas, and always had a good sense of comedy. She had never played in social or political comedy, but was enjoying the role of Mrs. Mister, the art-loving culture-vulture wife of Steeltown's boss. She said *Cradle* was as close as she had ever been to a strike in her life.

Olive Stanton was making her Broadway debut in a role that all actresses love to play—a prostitute. She was a Welles' find. He chose her for her fresh, innocent looks. He told her he did not want a brassy or hard-boiled girl for the part—in other words, the usual stage whore. He wanted just an ordinary American girl driven to sell her body because of the Depression; she could not get a job and was hungry. "He also liked me because he said I could take direction—and I do exactly what he tells me."

The role of Junior Junior, Mr. Mister's son, went to Hiram Sherman, a boyhood friend of Welles' from their native Wisconsin. He was ideal for the innocuous role of the young man who wants to be a journalist and sings the ditty, "Junior Wants to Go to Honolulu." Chubby, as he was called by Welles and Houseman, made his debut as an actor in their production of *'Tis Pity She's a Whore.*

The form of *Cradle* fell between Odets' *Waiting for Lefty* and *Threepenny Opera. Cradle* had the bare stage appeal of the first with the satiric punch of Brecht. Blitzstein used vignettes and flashbacks as Odets did in *Lefty* to develop his background and theme of corruption; for his finale he turned to the direct thrust of agitprop technique. Its style was a combination of vaudeville, declamation, and political satire. Some of its songs were patter, mock operetta, and others had the driving power of marching songs.

From the first audition, Flanagan visualized *Cradle* being produced on a bare stage like *Lefty.* Both she and Houseman wanted it done that way, but Welles had an elaborate show in mind. He asked the designer Ed Schruers to devise what Houseman described in his book as "an extravagant scenic scheme that called for . . . narrow, glass-bottomed, fluorescent platforms, loaded with scenery and props . . . as the scene shifted back and forth from night court, a doctor's office, and the front lawn of the finest home in Steeltown, USA."

Houseman called *Cradle* "America's first proletarian musical," but Blitzstein insisted that it was more middle-class than proletarian. For America is no land of peasants as some of the countries in Europe are; we have never had a tradition of peasantry in such a sense. They were dirt farmers, poor whites on the land, or blacks, mostly sharecroppers, with absentee landlords. And unlike most peasants in Europe they had the chance to rise and take their place in the middle class. Besides, most industrial workers belong to this broad social group.

But Houseman is right when he describes the course of

rehearsal of the musical at the Maxine Elliott. He wrote in his memoir: "Almost from the first day, there were strange, prophetic stirrings in the air—a turbulence grew with the weeks as the harsh realities of the national crisis met the rising theatrical excitement that was being generated on our bare, worklit stage."

As we got close to final rehearsals, rumors of cuts rose to a new high. In case of dismissals, Flanagan hoped to salvage some units so the project might continue on the basis of its accomplishments. Administrators and directors denied rumors of cuts to keep up some semblance of order and activity. Their denials did little to calm the fears of workers who had been jobless, known hunger, and again faced the despair of being out of work and having to haunt the relief bureau.

WPA workers had found a bit of security, some possibly for the first time in their lives. It was only human that they would try to hold on to the projects. Leaflets urged them not to accept a pink slip without a fight. Extremists, left and right, stirred up their fears to the point of panic. The press and conservative congressmen exploited the situation by calling project workers bums and boondogglers who had been coddled by the "socialistic" Roosevelt administration into believing that the country owed them a living.

By mid-May, though no official orders had gone out, unions were protesting the upcoming cuts. On May 19, the dance company of *How Long Brethren?* and *Candide* staged a sit-down as the curtain fell at the Nora Bayes. Charles Wiedman, as Candide, appeared on the stage to tell the audience about the cuts, and to ask as many as would to "sitdown" with them. A great cheer rose, I was recently told by Sam Chavkin, the dance press agent; he said that more than five hundred of the seven hundred remained in the theatre and started singing, "Hail, Hail, the Gang's All Here."

Around midnight 350 pickets arrived to march in front of the theatre on West 44th Street, chanting slogans which soon brought complaints from the Astor Hotel. Crowds formed, police rushed to the scene, and pickets from other projects showed up with makeshift placards. Friends brought food and blankets for the sitins and then joined the singing pickets. The demonstration went on till dawn when police ordered the dancers and audience out of the theatre; the protestors went out peacefully to be greeted by headlines in the morning papers.

To climax their protests of the rumored cuts, Arts project workers of New York City joined in a one-day, city-wide stoppage of all WPA on May 27. It was a general strike called by the American Federation of Labor, WPA Teachers' Union, Federation of Architects, Chemists and Technicians. Artists' Union, Workers' Alliance, Writers' Union, City Project Council, Project Supervisors' Council, and the American Newspaper Guild, of which I was a member.

Lookit, I'm paying 55¢ for standing room
and a week ago I could have seen the same dancers
on the picket line for nothing.

Act Three

Seven thousand on the Arts projects marched in the parade that marked the stoppage. It was led by the circus elephant with a banner hanging down its sides bearing the legend, "I'M ON MY WAY TO THE GLUE FACTORY." There was no singing of slogans, only placards and banners, calling for "No Cuts on WPA," "Jobs Not Relief," and "F.D.R. Keep Your Promise." That night all project theatres were dark. Flanagan checked the houses, saw police and guards stationed at all of them, and reported there was no violence or vandalism anywhere.

The next day Hallie was scheduled to speak before the National Theatre Council convening at the Astor Hotel. She was urged by friends not to mention the strike, but she was no person to ignore such an event. Flanagan told the group that project workers were "striking for what was once described as life, liberty, and the pursuit of happiness. . . . If we object to that method, I feel some word should come from this gathering as to a better method." No one objected.

Five blocks away, at the Maxine Elliott, I caught one of the final *Cradle* rehearsals. After Olive Stanton sang her street-walker's ballad, "Nickle Under the Foot," and "Chubby" Sherman went into his rollicking, "Junior Wants to Go to Honolulu," da Silva confronted Will Geer, the Steeltown boss, with the explosive theme song:

That's thunder, that's lightning,
And it's going to surround you!
No wonder those stormbirds
Seem to circle around you . . .

When you can't climb down,
And you can't sit still;
That's a storm
That's going to last until
The final wind blows . . .

And when the wind blows
The Cradle will rock!

143

25

CRADLE was too militant a show to be opening while the WPA was in danger and striking workers were making headlines. The most shocking headline was that of the Memorial Day Massacre of unarmed strikers and their families who faced five hundred Chicago police—their clubs, grenades, and guns—before the gates of Tom Girdler's Republic Steel. When Flanagan first heard the Blitzstein work that winter, it struck her as a perfect experimental project. As we neared the date of its first paid preview on June 16, its message sounded inflammatory, but she was busy on too many fronts to catch the danger signal.

Two other events occurred a few days apart before the stoppage. One was a march to Washington from New York and other eastern cities to present petitions asking for no cuts to WPA officials by unions that representated the majority of workers on the Arts projects. The other was the premiere of *Revolt of the Beavers,* a children's play which brought charges that Federal Theatre had produced a play to promote Communism among children.

Busloads of Federal One workers made the Washington trip. It was a warm day late in May; a thousand or more marched before WPA headquarters, chanting and carrying placards. A WPA spokesman took the petitions and promised to pass them on to the proper officials. On their way back the protestors stopped at Bel Air in Maryland, for a snack. Max Shohet told me that the café owner refused to serve a Negro in the group and ordered them all out; they rose to sing, "We Shall Not Be Moved." Then they marched out, boarded their bus, and returned to New York.

Revolt of the Beavers by Oscar Saul and Lou Lantz was directed by Elia Kazan. In the cast, as the leader of the beavers, was Jules Dassin, another young actor who was to become a film director. Makeup for the beavers was designed by Jay Williams who was general stage manager of the One-Act Experimental Theatre, and later author of *Stage Left,* an analysis of the left-wing theatre movement of the period.

Flanagan considered *Beavers* a fairy tale. It seemed natural to her that, in bringing it up to date, the beavers would face a bad king whom they had to drive out so that they could all "eat ice cream, play, and be nine years old." But Brooks Atkinson, who had been a friend of the project, connected the roller-skating beavers with Communism. He could not resist the quip that *Beavers* was "Marxism à la Mother Goose," though the Hearst *Journal-American* saw it as we did—a harmless and pleasing fantasy for children.

A noted psychologist, in charge of audience research, promptly reported that the play's social and political significance was over the children's heads and that they saw it simply as a tale about good and bad beavers. Its authors were quoted as saying, "If we hadn't put the word 'revolt' in the title, nobody would have raised an eyebrow about such significance."

Copies of Atkinson's *Times* review were sent to every congressman in Washington; no doubt the mailing was instigated by superpatriots on the project. Deputy Commissioner Brynes MacDonald, whose attention was also called to the review, announced that he was returning 1,400 tickets which the project had sent free for distribution by the Police Athletic League of New York City. The commissioner charged in *Variety* that the play attempted to "instill doctrines opposed to the democratic principles upon which this country was founded." Later *The Saturday Evening Post* editorialized that Federal Theatre was teaching poor children to hate— and possibly to murder—rich children.

Yet Hallie told her husband, Philip H. Davis, that *Beavers* was "very human and amusing and tragic and very class-conscious," according to Jane Mathews in *Federal Theatre.* (While researching her book in the sixties, Mathews had several interviews with Flanagan at an upstate New York nursing home before she died of Parkinson's disease in 1969.) Mathews wrote of *Beavers:* "Perhaps she expected Marxian overtones to go unnoticed. The play, she may have reasoned, was, after all, for the Children's Theatre. . . . [But it] opened at a time when the future of the entire WPA was once again up for debate."

In the May issue of *Fortune,* the project was praised for having brought about a cultural revolution. The article described the Living Newspaper as "applying to the stage the technique developed on the air and screen by the *March of Time,*" and that it had "created as much excitement among playwrights as among Republicans who saw its *Triple-A* and *Power* as government subsidized propaganda." The piece, probably written by Archibald MacLeish, the Pulitzer Prize poet-playwright who was on the staff of *Fortune* at the time, also said that "The Federal Theatre is a roaring success."

June 10, after weeks of debate in Washington, came the news of a thirty percent cut—1,700 theatre workers in New York. There were immediate protests and demonstrations by the City Projects Council and the Workers' Alliance. Sitdowns were called; at Harlem's Lafayette three hundred members of the Negro unit were joined by four hundred in the audience when the curtain went down on the recently opened *The Case of Philip Lawrence,* while pickets marched in front of the theatre.

By now rumors had reached Washington that *Cradle* was a "dangerous" show and should be checked before it opened to the public. Ellen Woodward, Federal One deputy, sent her executive assistant Lawrence Morris, a soft-voiced, brilliant literary man who had distinguished himself as a troubleshooter for the writers' project. Morris attended a runthrough of *Cradle* with Flanagan, who reported that he not only liked it but pronounced it "magnificent."

When I recently spoke with Morris at his East Side apartment, he still agreed that *Cradle* was a "magnificent" show, but added that he should have been more aware and critical of its significance at the time, considering that the Arts projects were in jeopardy and the nation was in industrial turmoil. He described Hallie as a forthright, impassioned woman who was impatient with politicians and bureaucracy but a dedicated teacher, director, and theatre woman, who respected talent and imagination and encouraged all of her workers to do their best. Describing an early visit to his office, Morris said that Hallie, on seeing a vase of wilted flowers on his desk, tossed them in the wastebasket, saying, "I can't stand those dead flowers!"

At that same interview I asked Morris about Colonel Somervell, archenemy of the Arts projects. Morris described him as "a mean, untrustworthy person, and I have no respect for him," and he added, "when delegations came to see him at the Armory, the colonel had a psychological advantage over them. The members of the project grievances committees had to sit on chairs that had their front legs cut down a bit; they kept slipping forward and this made them feel uneasy and unsure before the military autocrat. He became a general during World War II—being rewarded as General Douglas MacArthur had been for clearing out the Bonus Marchers in '32."

Four days before the first paid *Cradle* previews, the four Arts project national directors received a memo prohibiting "because of cuts and reorganization" any play, musical performance, or art gallery to open before July 1. "This was obviously censorship under a different guise," Flanagan said, as Farnsworth, Houseman, Welles, Virgil Thomson, and others tried to get *Cradle* an exception from the Washington order.

When they failed, Welles and MacLeish flew to Washington to see Hopkins. He was not available; they saw David Niles, head of WPA information, and Ellen Woodward, Federal One deputy. Niles, who had been involved with the *Ethiopia* ban, told them that *Cradle* was being postponed, not cancelled. Welles said that his protest was an artistic one, not political; and, if the government did not let the show open as scheduled, he and Houseman would launch it on their own.

"In that case," Niles said, "we would no longer be interested in it as a property."

Uncle Sam Presents

"So Jack Houseman and Orson Welles took the play down the street and . . . opened it as the first production of the Mercury Theatre," Flanagan wrote in *Arena.* "Probably it was worth a case of censorship to launch . . . our most brilliant directors and actors with a play for which the cast and rehearsal time had been provided . . . and an audience and a springboard for publicity."

Cradle gave its final run-through before an invited group of friends, WPA and Federal Theatre staffs. The audience was a cross section of musical and theatre people, along with such Broadway figures as Moss Hart, George S. Kaufman, and the producer Arthur Hopkins. I remember during the performance that Lehman Engel struggled with his twenty-eight men in the pit, that actors fumbled on the stage, and that Welles' ingenious, lit-up glass wagons had much to do with the general confusion. The show stood still until da Silva, wearing a dirty blond toupée, came forward with his exciting songs. But at the end there was no smell of a hit at the Maxine Elliott.

The next day WPA guards locked the theatre doors. At our information office the theatre party unit called the various organizations to announce the cancellation of *Cradle.* In the meantime, Houseman, Welles, and Blitzstein planned their strategy in the ladies' lounge of the theatre while the secretary, Augusta, informed the same organizations that the previews would take place as scheduled. Part of the strategy was to locate a theatre and find a piano so they could put on the show—without scenery, costumes, orchestra, chorus, and most of the cast.

At the press office I answered calls from columnists, editors, and other newsmen to confirm or deny what was going on at the Maxine Elliott. I repeated the official story, on orders from Mauntz and Davis. Unions called to say that they wanted no part of the runaway production—Actors Equity, American Federation of Musicians, and IATSE, the stagehands' union.

Except for some of the principals—Geer, da Silva, Sherman—most of the cast and chorus, all with relief status, could not appear in the show. Nor could I continue to publicize it. Houseman prevailed on his friend Helen Deutsch, then a Theatre Guild press agent, to call a press conference to say that *Cradle* would go on, even if Blitzstein had to sing all the roles—alone.

The group still had no theatre the day of the first preview. But that evening I joined the spirited audience that had come to see the show—assured that it would go on somewhere. Away from the office, I felt more loyal to *Cradle* than to the project. When I reached the dark Maxine Elliott around seven I found a big crowd there. Most of the people were part of the Downtown Music School theatre party. A sign plastered over the houseboard announced, "NO SHOW TONIGHT." That was when I noticed "Light*n*ing by Feder"—which turned out to be more appropriate for the occasion than "lighting."

As the crowd grew and spilled into 39th Street, police showed up to see whether there might be a disturbance. Geer came forward with an empty crate; he stood up on it and did a bit from the show and sang one of its songs. In reply to the question whether the show would go on, Geer, speaking like a country parson, said, "Sure as God made green apples." Then da Silva sang a song, and Chubby came on with his "I Want to Go to Honolulu." While they entertained the growing audience my friend George Zorn, who had been trying to locate a theatre for the show, showed up and told us that he had found the Venice at 58th and Seventh Avenue.

I was so caught up in the rush of events that I forgot I had been taken off the show. I rushed to a telephone booth and called the city desks of the newspapers and wire services—despite Uncle Sam's ban on it. When I got back to the Maxine Elliott, Geer was telling the crowd to join him and da Silva on a march to the Venice Theatre. I joined them walking alongside Geer, as we paraded up Seventh Avenue through the traffic and flashing lights of Times Square.

By the time we reached the theatre, a large crowd was in the lobby and the street. Hallie was not in sight, but police, the press, WPA officials, everybody else was there—except the United States Marines who should have been, since the runaway show was a sort of mutiny against the government. In the lobby Houseman introduced me to Helen Deutsch; I left them and went inside to stand at the back. The theatre was dusty and run-down; it had been used on some weekends by an Italian stock company. That accounted for the faded backdrop of the Bay of Naples and an Italian flag hanging from an upper box.

As an old upright piano was being rolled into position on one side of the stage, Feder adjusted lights and spots. One of the spots lit up the red, white, and green flag. The audience, aware and indignant about what Mussolini had done to Ethiopia and was then doing in Spain, started to boo and yell. Someone in a lower box climbed up and ripped it down. The audience cheered.

About nine o'clock Blitzstein walked on the bare stage and sat before the piano. The audience greeted him with a burst of applause. Houseman and Welles came onstage and took their places, Welles at one end and Houseman at the center. Houseman spoke first, telling them about *Cradle*'s problems and thanking Flanagan and the Federal Theatre for letting them put it on as their own show. Welles, looking youthful but tired, set the scene and told of the principal characters involved in the plot. Then he introduced Blitzstein and turned the show over to him.

The handsome, swarthy-looking composer, in shirtsleeves and suspenders, was picked up by a spot as he played the notes of the opening song. After he sang a few words, a faltering soprano voice joined him. A breathless sound rose through the house as a spot picked up Olive Stanton in a lower box, making her debut in a green dress and scared as hell. That was the first of a number of surprises, as principals rose, sang, or spoke from the aisles, the boxes, and the audience, while Blitzstein kept beating the piano and singing with more showmanship and excitement than any twenty-eight piece orchestra in the pit.

This was the only way the show could go on without violating union regulations. Luckily, it was the only way to do the show, as Hallie had seen it in her mind's eye, without cluttering it up with scenery, costumes, and other trappings, such as Welles' glass-bottomed wagons. And da Silva was more in character as Larry Foreman, the workers' hero, without his blond wig (which was locked up at the Maxine Elliott) as he sang the thundering finale:

> When you can't climb down,
> And you can't sit still . . .
> And when the wind blows
> The Cradle will rock!

It was an inspired theatre performance with the added thrill of being a runaway show. Houseman called it Broadway's first "happening," and the papers reported it as a news event instead of a theatrical premiere. The next morning Blitzstein, Welles, and Houseman were on the front page of all the papers and woke up to find themselves famous. And I, the project press agent, lost my first Broadway show—one that was to become a milestone in American theatre history.

26

THE *Cradle* controversy was to mark a turning point in Washington from the liberal WPA policy of the early New Deal to the appeasement of conservative forces which demanded cuts in relief funds, a tougher stand toward labor, and a firmer control of Federal Theatre. For, despite its successes, or perhaps, because of them and the charges of radicalism and propaganda, the project was increasingly becoming a liability to Roosevelt's overall social program.

With every advance toward a nationwide people's theatre, Flanagan saw what she called in her memoir, "the rising fear of persons who did not want that kind of theatre. What might have been called the cultural fear of the Arts projects was expressed publicly by Walter Damrosch and Otis Skinner, who shunned the thought of perpetuating any form of art which had grown out of the groundwork of relief." In this connection she had to assure the American National Theatre and Academy (ANTA) that the Federal Theatre had no designs on the name or their aims for a national theatre.

The conservative trend was in accord with the cultural era of Maude Adams and Otis Skinner—the era when the four hundred in furs and jewels were the patrons of the theatre. Flanagan had been pushing for a more democratic audience. She saw the Arts projects as "America's protest against a too thin-blooded culture. If they achieved art, it was the result of people working imaginatively ... in relation to problems and communities" which the audience understood and shared.

Though there was always the question, "Was the primary emphasis of the project on relief or the theatre?" Flanagan insisted that it was a work project as a temporary relief program. "It was perhaps the greatest handicap of the Arts project," she said in *Arena,* "that WPA . . . never succeeded in explaining to the public that when people came into the projects they were no longer relief clients, but people doing work useful enough to be paid out of government funds," like anyone else working for Uncle Sam.

During the 30 percent cuts that summer, which dropped 1,400 from the New York City payroll, amid protests, sit-downs, and other demonstrations, the WPA bureaucracy announced another drastic change in line with the trend to the right. The *Federal Theatre Magazine* was ordered to cease publication. Ostensibly it was for lack of funds, but Flanagan and others believed that it was a continuation of the censorship that had stemmed from *Cradle.* The last issue came out June 14, 1937.

Toward the end it appeared sporadically like the old *Bulletin* but it had proved popular with colleges, universities, little theatres, and schools throughout the nation. Still free to project workers and tax-supported institutions, it was on sale in more than a hundred bookshops and newsstands at fifteen cents a copy. When Flanagan was asked by a Washington official, why there was a theatre magazine and not one for the other arts, she considered the question an indirect attack on the theatre project.

When she was asked whether the magazine was sold at workers' bookstores, Hallie said yes, along with Brentano's, Gotham Book Mart, and a hundred other bookshops and newsstands. Wasn't its editor Pierre de Rohan a Communist? She replied that de Rohan was a Democrat, a World War veteran, and had been recommended to her by the then Vice President John Garner. Wasn't there too much emphasis on poor people in shirtsleeves and audiences in the park? Was that the *kind* of audiences for government shows?

Then she was asked about a quotation on the inside cover of the spring issue in 1937 of *Federal Theatre Magazine.* I recently checked the lines; they were quoted from *The Dog Beneath the Skin,* a poetic play by W. H. Auden and Christopher Isherwood. They had been used, she explained, with the aim of encouraging directors, designers, playwrights, and others to do their best: "The precision of your instruments and the skill of your designers is unparalleled / Unite. / Your knowledge and your power are capable of infinite extension: / Act."

Flanagan was aware that literary references were regarded with suspicion by Washington officials. Such references were now dangerous—with the 1935 social and labor policies of WPA being reversed in 1937. Washington seemed displeased with her and Farnsworth for not having handled the 30 percent cuts in a more ruthless manner. With the help of Charles Ryan, the personnel director, they had set up a friendly procedure of meeting delegations that protested the cuts and managed the 1,400 dismissals without major disorders.

It appeared that Washington no longer wanted the plays and the magazine to represent the expression of those on the project or continue as "the show window of the WPA." For the administration was now having serious trouble: the political coalition which had reelected Roosevelt by a landslide in 1936 was falling apart because of his Supreme Court fight and the heavy congressional attacks on his social and economic programs.

One of the conservatives' main targets was Harry Hopkins and his WPA "extravagances." His request for 1938 funds before the Congressional Appropriations Committee did not come without tighter controls, and his salary was cut from $12,000 to $10,000 a year. The new political coalition called for getting rid of the radical image of the Arts projects. To Washington the projects needed a tough, conservative boss in New York.

Without consulting the national directors, Washington sent Paul Edwards, now of the WPA finance division, to "clean up" New York and administer the arts. His job was to replace Farnsworth, who supervised Federal Theatre, and Harold Stein, who had been lenient also in dealing with the 30 percent cuts on the other projects. With Edwards in charge of finance, employment, labor, and supply, Flanagan realized that she would lose control of the project.

She appealed to Hopkins; he was out of town. Then she called Ellen Woodward who said she could do nothing about the appointment. Woodward was the daughter of a Mississippi judge and did as she was told by her superiors. Other national directors were upset; they even spoke of resigning, but decided against it. Under the circumstances Washington would have welcomed their resignations and turned the arts back to the states. Farnsworth was forced to resign; he was a great loss to Flanagan as they had worked together harmoniously that year.

Following an appeal by Flanagan to cooperate with Edwards, the directors stayed on and started the job of reorganizing their units. But Walter Hart, head of New York City productions, who had gone through nine reorganizations in eighteen months, would not face another and quit. At the same time Flanagan was unable to reengage John Houseman, who was now available; he was a British citizen and WPA would not exempt him from the new congressional order barring aliens from working on relief projects.

Flanagan sought to replace Hart with Farnsworth as head of New York productions. Though she got Equity to approve his name before submitting it to Washington, Woodward refused to clear Farnsworth without Hopkins' permission and he was now on vacation. Flanagan stood helpless as she saw the project being "practically wrecked." That summer *Variety* reported that "a purge" was in the wings, and that Flanagan might not survive.

Her other choice for the post was George Kondolf, the New York producer who headed the Chicago project. His qualifications were right for the new trend: he was a professional theatre man, worked well with bureaucrats, was a Catholic and an outspoken conservative. With such a background Kondolf might offset charges of radicalism on the New York project. On taking the post Kondolf retained Philip Barber as head of the productions board and brought in three new directors, James R. Ullman, Charles Freeman, and Morris Ankrum, to fill vacant posts.

In late August, 1937, Flanagan turned labor relations, finances, everything but artistic policy and personnel over to Edwards. Soon afterwards he asked her to attend a meeting with Equity and the Workers' Alliance to iron out their differences. Flanagan faced Burgess Meredith, acting president of Equity, and Willie Morgan, head of the Alliance, and urged them to quit fighting, get their members behind Edwards, and restore the morale of the previous year. Despite charges by Morgan that Edwards' job was to kill the projects, she persuaded him and Meredith to work with the new regime and get shows going again.

It was unfortunate for Flanagan that 1937 was a bad year for Hopkins. Both he and his wife had cancer; she was to die that fall. After her death, which dealt a severe blow to Hopkins, he guessed his own ailment and went to the Mayo Clinic for tests and an operation. He did not return until the spring of 1938. This made it necessary for him to hand over control of the Arts projects to his deputy Ellen Woodward. To help her steer them toward the new conservative trend was David Niles, the WPA information officer who had been responsible for the suppression of *Ethiopia* and *The Cradle Will Rock*.

The night before Hopkins left for Mayo, looking haggard and scarred from many political battles, he said to Flanagan: "I'm sorry about not having seen you oftener. You have done a big job. Nobody knows how big, and I'm grateful. I want you to know it and, if you can stand it, I want you to keep on during the hard days ahead. We mustn't lose the ground we've gained."

Being devoted to Hopkins, Hallie now blamed the new Washington bureaucracy for placing her in an impossible position on the project. Without the support of his crusading spirit, she was lost and the project was bound to suffer. Flanagan could not believe she had done anything but what Hopkins had encouraged her to do, namely to do some relevant plays on the current scene. Though she shared his crusades, she lacked Hopkins' political sense, and she did not realize that the idealistic social worker had to become a politician in order to win his reforms. Hopkins was loyal to his overall aims of WPA, she to those of a people's theatre.

Flanagan knew that such a theatre might at times appear

controversial and even radical, depending on one's politics, but Hopkins had given her the green light in 1935 when he pledged "a free, adult, uncensored theatre." That this sort of theatre was no longer in favor struck Flanagan as a rejection of her ideals, which she saw as the basis for a nationwide people's theatre.

"Like many thoroughly dedicated individuals," Jane Mathews declared "Flanagan had to pursue that to which she was committed whole-heartedly. Anything less would have seemed almost a violation of her own integrity, a threat to the kind of theatre she was laboring to build. Her zeal, neither politic, bureaucratic, nor 'safe,' was the kind of zeal that turned a relief project into a theatre. It was also the kind of zeal that made bureaucrats shudder."

27

 EARLY in the summer of 1937, Hopkins was still around to
help Hallie. He told her to carry on, despite the chaos of cuts,
reorganization, and the political trend, with her overall program that included the Caravan Theatre. That unit was my
temporary assignment, after losing *Cradle;* I assisted James
Hughes in publicizing it until I was assigned a new show of
my own.

The Caravan fleet of five big trucks that opened out into
complete stages presented Shakespeare, Gilbert and Sullivan, variety shows, and plays to thousands under the stars
for free. In addition to covering the press, Jim and I had to
catch performances in the five boroughs: the Mall in Central
Park and Washington Square in Manhattan; Prospect Park
in Brooklyn; Highland Park in Queens; Owl's Head in Bay
Ridge; St. Mary's Park in the Bronx; and Silver Lake in Staten
Island.

Together we attended a performance of *Melodies on Parade,* a nostalgic vaudeville revue, in Washington Square,
against the shadow of the graceful Washington Arch. We
noticed that the audience came from all parts of Greenwich
Village, students and professors of New York University and
ritzy Fifth Avenue, and immigrant families that had settled
in the area since the turn of the century.

It was a lively and informal three thousand or more, sitting
on benches or on the grass, babes in mothers' arms, men
fanning themselves with straw hats, kids scampering about
until the musicians sounded the overture, then sitting cross-
legged on the ground to watch the show. They were silent
and enthralled while the veteran showmen sang, danced,
and did their comic routines. The end was greeted with resounding cheers and whistles, and cries of "More, more!"

Act Three

Family Circle

The only person who has done this audience justice is Don Freeman in his sketch, "Family Circle," which captures the meaning of a people's theatre: Hallie's aim for all America.

"Properly speaking these are festivals," wrote Atkinson of the Caravan shows in the *Times*. "A mass of children is crowding as close to the ropes as the law will permit; young legs protrude from under the spotlight platform and dangle out of the trees. When the warning lights go up, they are the ones that cheer, clap, and whistle; and when the play finally begins in the twilight, they all move forward as though something had pushed them. Eagerness can move a crowd as one man."

As we followed the caravans from park to park the Gilbert and Sullivan productions became our favorites. In makeshift costumes the performers first struggled and then mastered the intricate patterns of the language, while the appreciative crowds smiled and then applauded. Where else, I wondered, could you hear the complex sounds of *Iolanthe* and *Pinafore* flavored by such accents—Jewish, Greek, Italian, Brooklynese—sometimes all together in a single chorus?

The New York *Post* editorialized: "While the experts of the theatre assembled in convention last week mourned the plight of the 'legitimate stage,' the Federal Theatre has quietly gone ahead and provided five companies of strolling players to put on outdoor shows throughout the boroughs. The experts came to no conclusion as to how to bring people into the theatre. But WPA seems to have accomplished much the same result by bringing the theatre to the people."

That summer also commemorated the 350th anniversary of the first English colony in the New World and a community venture was shaping up in North Carolina which would play an important part in my career. It was Paul Green's historical pageant, *The Lost Colony,* which told in words, music, and dance the heroic but tragic drama of Sir Walter Raleigh's first settlement in the New World. WPA and other agencies, in cooperation with state and local historical associations, had rebuilt Fort Raleigh with a hand-hewn stockade, chapel, fort, and cabins in the spirit of the original colony of 1587 on the Carolina coast.

An outdoor theatre was built on a slope leading to Roanoke Sound for the presentation of the spectacle. The production was supervised by Frederick Koch and directed by Samuel Selden, both of the Carolina Playmakers. Flanagan had arranged for New York City project actors to play the principal roles in the large cast. Elizabethan songs were researched by Green; one that underscored the milkmaids' dance, was "Greensleeves." Though mentioned in *The Merry Wives of Windsor* and tremendously popular in Shakespeare's time, "Greensleeves" then "passed from remembrance," according to a recent note from Green, and it was *The Lost Colony* that "helped to reestablish it in the world." I was fascinated by the project especially when Flanagan and President Roosevelt journeyed there for the celebration of Virginia Dare's birthday, but my own summer was full of new assignments and I did not anticipate that I would shortly become an integral part of *The Lost Colony*.

On June 19, forty directors, actors, designers, and technicians from projects all over the nation gathered at Vassar for a six-week course in theatre training, sponsored by the Rockefeller Foundation, the government, and the college. Flanagan had spoken of cancelling the session because of project cuts, but Hopkins persuaded her to go on with it. The forty theatre people were chosen by their regional directors; the object of the session was to learn by producing a new play.

The play chosen was the new Living Newspaper, *One-Third of a Nation,* as a sort of pre-Broadway tryout. It was written by Arthur Arent, who wrote *Power.* Howard Bay was chosen to design the set, which consisted of a broken staircase, bits of crumbling walls, a fire escape, a leaky sink, and a toilet seat hanging from the flies. The set aimed to suggest rather than show the run-down state of slum tenements and their relationship to poverty, crime, and disease.

Daily courses were given in every phase of theatre. Madalyn O'Shea ran an acting laboratory; Tamiris directed body movement classes; Mary Merrill showed costumes being put together; Arent explained how the Living Newspaper was researched and written. Feder demonstrated his basic twelve-lamp hookup and how it varied for different kinds of shows. When we complained that Feder used too many lights, he would say, "Don't buy flats, paint, or costumes. Buy lights!"

Hallie invited me to spend a day at Vassar to observe the sessions and give me a new assignment: the project's revival of John Howard Lawson's *Processional,* which was first presented in 1925 by the Theatre Guild starring George Abbott and June Walker. *Processional* was one of the first plays of the American social scene: a West Virginia mining town in the throes of a strike. It showed workers marching for a better life, and was stylized like a vaudeville to the jazz tempo of the twenties.

"Lawson's doing a new version for us," she said. "See how it differs from the original."

When I returned to the Maxine Elliott, *Processional* was

rehearsing under Lem Ward's direction. Earl Robinson, a young project composer, had written a new jazz score that was more in the folk jazz idiom than of vaudeville. In the leading roles were Ruth Gilbert as Sadie and George Mathews, now a film and television actor, as Dynamite Jim. The large cast included Isabel Bonner and her husband Joseph Kramm, who later wrote *The Shrike.*

After the Broadway premiere of *Marching Song,* Lawson returned to his chores in Hollywood, where I contacted him about *Processional* changes. He wrote me that the script was almost the same, except for eliminating some vaudeville routines and making the characters less stereotyped. Though the bosses and troopers struck me as the fascists of 1925, they were less caricatured than in the original, and the miners

Mrs. Eleanor Roosevelt, Playwright Paul Green, and
Producer D.B. Fearing.

were shown as hard-working Americans with no propaganda slant.

The revival opened that fall and was well received. Wolcott Gibbs wrote in *The New Yorker* that *"Processional* is a brutal fantasy about the West Virginia miners, in which characters, stylized and grotesque, move always to the beat of contemporary jazz." Howard Barnes in the *Herald Tribune:* "The Federal Theatre production has an emotional thrust . . . that makes the current Broadway exhibits seem extremely anemic by comparison." It played 81 performances to the Theatre Guild's 105 at the old Garrick Theatre.

I invited John Dos Passos, Lawson's friend, to attend because he had seen the Guild production. He wrote Lawson: "Dawn [Powell] and I saw *Processional.* It's amazing how well it holds up. The production is excellent. . . . The general tone is much less brilliant and cute than the Theatre Guild production . . . but the underlying struggle got over much better. It seemed to me damned stirring and it certainly stirred the audience. The musical score is excellent—in tone with the general charcoal drawing effect. . . . I was very much pepped up by seeing it and feel a certain vague interest in the theatre—which for a long time has caused me only disgust —reawaking."

For all its "emotional thrust" and melodramatic power, however, *Processional* seemed to me unreal, dated, and romanticized. Too much had happened on the labor scene since the twenties, and *The Cradle Will Rock* had more effectively presented the spirit and violence of the new industrial era in its satiric song and dance. Playing the Maxine Elliott where *Cradle* rehearsed and never opened, I had the strange feeling that it was simply a weak replacement for the Blitzstein work. Perhaps because I was close to both shows, I was disappointed in *Processional.* In spite of its social message and driving intensity, it shuffled along as a cross between a jazzy vaudeville and a stylized expressionistic piece of the experimental twenties that defied being updated.

The Vassar tryout of *One-Third of a Nation* led to several productions that winter. In addition to the version done in

New York, it was presented with changes to meet local housing conditions in New Orleans, Detroit, Philadelphia, Seattle, and other cities. Reviewing the Cincinnati production Edward Carberry wrote: "One of the very rare things in the theatre: a play which makes an important subject tremendously interesting."

For the New York City production, which opened January 17, 1938, Howard Bay redesigned the set. He now used the cross-section of a real slum tenement that could go up in flames nightly at the Adelphi. Though it differed from the Vassar set, its symphonic integration of music, movement, and theme was heightened. Burns Mantle said in the *Daily News:* "The most interesting of the Living Newspaper series . . . as fine a setting as any stage this town has ever shown." Sidney Whipple in the *World-Telegram:* "A human document . . . in a setting which for stark realism has never been surpassed."

One-Third of a Nation was a vivid history of housing conditions and battles between tenants and landlords during the past hundred years. Arthur Arent wrote a fully-documented and dramatic script; it was directed by Lem Ward, who had staged *Processional.* The production struck me as less stylized but no less poetic than the previous Living Newspapers, and got its message across with the raw realism of the times. I could smell the roaches, the overflowing garbage, and the dank air within the old tenement walls, like those I had known as a boy living in the Lower East Side of Little Italy.

I cheered with the packed house when the crumbling, rat-infested slum was engulfed in flames and smoke at the end. Many in the audience had lived or were still living in such tenements and were expecting help from the Federal government's low-rent housing program. But its budget, according to Mayor LaGuardia, was "only a drop in the bucket"; and the "Consumer," comparing the sum to that for the military, said that Uncle Sam spent more money "to kill a man than to keep him alive." The Consumer's last words were a call to action, as fiery as the blaze that mushroomed onstage: "Can you hear me, Washington? Give me a decent home!"

Act Three

Along with Kurt Weill, Paul Green, Herman Shumlin, and President MacCracken of Vassar, Eleanor Roosevelt declared that *One-Third of a Nation* achieved "something which will mean a tremendous amount in the future, socially, and in the education and growing-up of America . . . far more than any amount of speeches by Langdon Post or I—or even the President—might make."

That June the script was sold to an independent film maker, who made the picture and released it through Paramount. The $5,000 from its sale was given to the American Newspaper Guild Committee for the Federal Writers project publications. It was a nonprofit group headed by Heywood Broun, Franklin P. Adams, Lewis Mumford, and others. The script, along with five other Federal Theatre plays, was published by Random House.

A sidelight of this Living Newspaper was a discussion in the Senate, in which Senator Josiah Bailey of North Carolina read parts of the script into the *Congressional Record.* Senator William Borah of Idaho asked Senator Wagner of New York, sponsor of the housing bill in Congress, "Why do we have these awful degraded conditions?" Senator Wagner replied, "It is because of the low incomes received by those who live in them. . . . If we overnight increased their incomes by a more fair distribution of the wealth of the country, we would not have any slums."

Senator C. O. Andrews of Florida then asked Wagner: "Where do the people who live in slums come from?" To which Wagner replied: "What does the Senator mean, 'Where do they come from?' Whether they come from foreign countries?" Senator Andrews explained: "I think we ought not to offer any inducement to people to come in from our country or foreign countries . . . to take advantage of our government supplying them with homes. . . . Examine the birth records of New York. Most of those in the slums weren't born there."

One-Third of a Nation, like most plays on a controversial subject, made more congressional enemies than friends. Aubrey Williams, a deputy WPA administrator, complained to

165

Flanagan that he had received reports that it had offended some senators. She replied, "If Senators and Congressmen oppose appropriations for housing and say so in Congress, why should they object to being quoted in the play?"

"Living Newspapers made enemies that were very powerful and instrumental in the closing of the project," Flanagan wrote in *Arena.* "I think of this fact at times and wonder whether it would have been better for the people on our project to have remained aloof from all subjects controversial. Then I realized that this would have barred from our stages, judging by the plays which involved us in censorship, Aristophanes, Shakespeare, Ben Jonson, Maxwell Anderson, Elmer Rice, Paul Green, and many other important authors classical and modern."

28

FEDERAL THEATRE's third season began with New York City in the throes of retrenchment and reorganization of all units. Though smaller projects in the country were shuttered, the rest of the nation for the first time overshadowed the big city. Its schedule was reduced from eighty to forty productions; few were in rehearsal or in the shops, and opening dates were being postponed, due to the slowing down of all activities.

The slowing down was expected, yet several directors, members of the Projects Supervisors Council, blamed most of the inactivity on the new adminstration. They appealed to Flanagan, saying that there was a conspiracy in Washington to sabotage the projects; and that Edwards had been sent quietly to kill off the Federal Theatre. Flanagan, always loyal to the administration, requested them, particularly Edward Goodman and Morris Watson as heads of the council, to cooperate with Edwards and keep up their good work.

New York announced productions to participate in the nationwide cycles and programs. Children's plays such as *A Hero Is Born* and *Treasure Island,* a Marionette Festival, and religious plays for Christmas. A series of dance productions: Doris Humphrey-Charles Weidman's *To the Dance, With My Red Fires,* and *Race for Life;* Tamiris' *The Trojan Incident,* a new version of Euripides' *Trojan Women,* translated by Professor Davis, Flanagan's husband, and the American premiere of Shaw's latest comedy *On The Rocks,* which was considered a Federal Theatre coup. Hallie was fond of Shaw who, like Eugene O'Neill, had granted her permission to do cycles of his plays throughout the country. "As long as you can stick to your fifty-five cent maximum for admission . . . you can have anything of mine," Shaw told her. "Any author of serious plays who does not follow my lead does not know what is good for him. I am not making a public-spirited offer; I am jumping at a good offer."

After *Processional* I was assigned to publicize *On the Rocks.* It was a long, talky play set in England of the early thirties and dealt with a conflict among political factions. I read the script and sat through rehearsals, yet no one, Edward Goodman, the producer, or Lucius Cook, the director, could be sure what Shaw was up to. The Prime Minister in his many discussions was trying to solve the Depression with a scheme that called for extreme measures—nationalization of land, abolition of taxes, and compulsory labor. The workers rejected his plan and England remained "on the rocks."

It seemed that Shaw, the old-line Socialist, thought his people wanted a dictatorship; he did not give it to them in the play despite the Prime Minister's vague prophecy of a strong man who will come to change the situation by force. There were rioting masses at the end of the play, but Shaw brought down the curtain before the mob broke more than a few windows. Though he gave a serious yet amusing analysis of England in economic chaos, he did not advocate the barricades. *On the Rocks* was everything—Communist, Socialist, capitalist, fascist—but most of all it was a bore.

None of us were bored by its fine cast. Harry Irvine, the star of *Murder in the Cathedral,* was back after a Hollywood stint, to play the Prime Minister. Estelle Winwood, one of the great ladies of high comedy, was cast as the Mysterious Lady in Grey. Two young actors stood out: Joseph Anthony, who was to become a Broadway director, and pretty Ardis Gaines, later Brenda Marshall in Hollywood.

Before *On the Rocks* opened at Daly's on June 15, after a couple of postponements, Producer Goodman and Director Cook had resigned from the project. Along with Morris Watson, they gave their reasons in a pamphlet, *Murder in the Federal Theatre,* accusing Edwards of being part of a Washington conspiracy to kill the project. James R. Ullman replaced Goodman as producer of the Shaw play, and Robert Ross restaged it.

Act Three

The pamphlet, endorsed by the Project Supervisors Council, was sold on newsstands. When Edwards failed to answer the charges, the council made other allegations which appeared in the press. Flanagan was upset by the controversy within the project. Commenting on it in *Arena,* she said, "Insecurity increased and with it jealousies between the two warring minority groups, the militants and the diehards . . . with apparently suicidal intent. . . . The worst morale we ever had on Federal Theatre."

In February 1938, I joined six supervisors and about eighty project workers in presenting a petition to Edwards, asking that he make no further cuts in relief personnel. It was a peaceful protest but *on project time.* Edwards ordered seven of us fired on the spot and the workers docked an hour's pay. The Project Supervisors Council took up our case, making a lively issue of "The Seven Who Were Hanged." The Newspaper Guild, of which I was a member, joined in the protests, along with the City Projects Council and Workers' Alliance.

After we took part in weeks of protest marches and meetings in dingy cold halls, Edwards quietly reinstated us. During that depressing time of being a casuality of cuts and dismissals, I had no intention of bothering Hallie who was busy with real problems from coast to coast. Though she might have approved of my act, I wrote her that I had to join in the protest and I didn't expect her to try and rescue me.

I was advised by friends that since Federal Theatre was bound to end someday, this was as good a time as any for me to see whether I could survive as a freelance writer in the big city. I hesitated, once more thinking of Hallie and her efforts to get me on the project, the Federal Theatre history that might never be finished for her, and my friends who were taking theatre to the millions. And yet, at the same time, I had a feeling that the project had seen its best days.

Half-heartedly I wrote and called people I had met through *Contempo* and was happy none of them could help me. But to keep myself busy, I took on a book column I had done previously and toyed with the idea of doing personality features for out-of-town newspapers. Calling myself the National Features Service, I had stationery printed, I queried editors on "exclusive" hometown stories, and soon was in business.

I received no pay for the column, only the review copies of the books, and I did what many struggling writers were doing: we took the books down to Schulte's on lower Fourth Avenue and received one-fourth of the list price in cash. Once a week I went downtown with an armful of books, swapped literary gossip with friends who were doing the same, and returned to pay the overdue rent. Mr. Pesky paid off quicker than a pawnbroker: we called him "the patron saint of freelancers."

After writing features for a single newspaper I hit on a syndication idea which made it possible for me to sell an "exclusive," with minor changes, to dozens of papers. The idea occurred to me one day as I strolled by the Radio City Music Hall and gazed at a blowup of the Rockettes—the trademark of that entertainment palace. When I saw the press agent, she was ready to cooperate, thus becoming my "legman" by supplying me with "cheesecake art" and the information I needed for the stories.

With the list of fifty or sixty Rockettes, their names and addresses, I queried editors of their home town papers, many of which were in big cities, offering them exclusive features with pictures of their own Rockettes. As orders came, I prepared a routine feature: I wrote two or three paragraphs about the local dancer, the rest was a canned story about the backstage life of the Rockettes and the opportunities for young dancers in this unique American precision ensemble at the Radio City Music Hall.

The papers paid promptly and I was rewarded with a year's pass to the Music Hall which I used once—to get out of the rain—and then gave it to a friend. Bored with this game, I contacted publishers and magazines about editorial work. Bennett Cerf and John Farrar were kind to reply that they had nothing that might interest me; George Stevens, then editor of the *Saturday Review,* engaged me to write a series on the writers I had known during *Contempo* days. I had time to do one: an article on William Faulkner which

Act Three

Trademark design by Elmer Hall in 1938 for *The Lost Colony*.

was featured on the cover and was to become a primary source on the Mississippi author's early career.

Though I had been reinstated on the project and could have returned to *On the Rocks,* I accepted Paul Green's offer to become national press representative of *The Lost Colony,* which was to begin its second season on Roanoke Island early that summer. Green told me that the islanders of the Outer Banks had been isolated from the mainland until the recent construction of a bridge. This explained the fact that the president of the local historical group that sponsored his pageant had asked him to make an odd request.

"Isolated all these years from the outside world," Green said, "there's something clannish about this Carolina folk. Their names are old English and their speech is quaint. They say 'oiland' for 'island,' and most of them have never been off it—except to fish—or have ever known a foreigner."

Green ran a hand through his wavy dark hair and went on

with an embarrassed smile: "Brad Fearing, who runs the island, is all for having you. But he asked me to find out if you'd mind changing your name to 'Butler.' I know you won't do it."

Dream of The Lost Colony

For here once walked the men of dreams,
The sons of hope and pain and wonder,
Upon their foreheads truth's bright diadem,
The light of the sun in their countenance,
And their lips singing a new song—
A song for ages yet unborn,
For us the children that came after them—
"O new and mighty world to be!"
They sang,
"O land majestic, free, unbounded!"

This was the vision, this the fadeless dream—
Tread softly, softly now these yellow stricken sands.
This was the grail, the living light that leapt—
Speak gently, gently on these muted tongueless shores.

Now down the trackless hollow years
That swallowed them but not their song
We send response—
"O lusty singer, dreamer, pioneer,
Lord of the wilderness, the unafraid,
Tamer of darkness, fire and flood,
Of the soaring spirit winged aloft
On the plumes of agony and death—
Hear us, O hear!
The dream still lives,
It lives, it lives,
And shall not die!"

—*Paul Green*

He then assured me that the job was mine. I went to work preparing an advance campaign for the new season. Before

Act Three

Eleanor Roosevelt riding in the truck to see *The Lost Colony* at the Waterside Theatre on Roanoke Island.

going to Roanoke Island, I planted stories, pictures, and layouts with syndicates. I met the New York actors and had them interviewed on network radio about the Lost Colony and the island as "the Birthplace of the Nation" and—across the sound where the Wright Brothers made their historic flight at Kitty Hawk—as "the Birthplace of Aviation."

When I stepped off the bus in front of the Dare County courthouse on Roanoke Island, I was met by Brad Fearing and his tobacco-chewing cronies. "Doggone it, it's good to have you," he said, introducing them to me. "I can't say your name. I hope you don't mind if we just call you Mr. Tony."

Brad set me up in the courthouse. I tackled the job inspired by their aim: to make the island a seashore resort and *The*

Uncle Sam Presents

Lost Colony an annual event. "I soon met Alf Drinkwater, the lanky, eagle-eyed, telegrapher who had tapped out the message of the historic passage to the New York *Herald*. When the editor called back to verify the story, because his roving reporter loved the bottle, Alf wired him, "your man was cold sober and so was I." I invited newsmen and critics to spend a few days with us. They came from Boston, Detroit, Philadelphia, Washington, along with five Broadway critics: Brooks Atkinson, *Times;* Burns Mantle, *Daily News;* Louis Kronenberger, *Time;* Robert Coleman, *Daily Mirror,* and Hobe Morrison, *Variety;* and photographers from *Life, Sunday News,* and *Paramount News*.

We took them fishing, swimming, sailing, rolling down the dunes, and picking baskets of cape jasmine, known elsewhere as gardenias, which they prized as souvenirs. They all raved about our outdoor show and primitive island wonderland. Brad Fearing praised the job I did, but it was not until my publicity story in a southern magazine was bought and condensed in *Reader's Digest* that he learned to "say" my full name.

29

WHILE Paul Edwards kept the project comparatively inactive during his first year, sporadic strikes and protest demonstrations continued to plague him and George Kondolf, the New York City director. Pickets paraded before Edwards' office on Madison Avenue and that of Kondolf's on the West Side. They also picketed Kondolf's house on lower Fifth Avenue, carrying signs and yelling slogans which called him a "hatchet man" of the Federal Theatre. When I recently saw Kondolf there, he showed me some old signs that the pickets had left which he had stored in the basement as souvenirs.

During the production inactivity of that winter, Flanagan took off to see what was happening on the West Coast. The shows she saw, seemed to compensate for the lack of activity in the East. In Los Angeles the team which had created *Follow the Parade* prepared another winner, *Ready! Aim! Fire!,* a musical satire on dictatorships which pointed the finger at no one in particular—European or Latin-American.

When she reached San Diego, telegrams, letters, and telephone calls caught up with her. Flanagan heard of labor problems in Hartford, script troubles in Jacksonville and Chicago, and big and small ones in New York. From Washington she got a mysterious-sounding message: "Office moving to Ouray Building." She soon learned that the Arts projects were being booted out of the run-down elegances of the McLean Mansion and into the shabby old structure of the Ouray Building—signifying a comedown for Federal One in the Washington spectrum.

Shortly after her return in January 1938, Flanagan and the three other national directors were called into Ellen Woodward's office and told that the arts in California were reverting to Colonel Donald Connolly, the army man who did not care for the arts and believed that the best project was one that "kept out of the papers." Flanagan, again loyal to the administration, pledged her support to the colonel and instructed her California directors to do likewise.

The moment the colonel's army bureaucracy took charge of the West Coast, project directors were forbidden to communicate with Flanagan, except through his office. All letters to directors and supervisors were opened. Gilmor Brown was dismissed as director, without the colonel notifying Flanagan. All scripts were called in; Elmer Rice's *Judgment Day,* set for early production, was cancelled with no explanation. These acts shocked Flanagan and the other national directors, who were also affected by the colonel's military takeover in California.

His dictatorial acts brought protests in the film capital from Actors Equity and the Screen Writers' Guild, along with other organizations and prominent figures. Even *Variety,* the show-biz trade journal, took up the cause of the Federal Theatre. Burgess Meredith, acting head of Equity, denounced the WPA administration's tendency to hire people for theatre jobs who were not qualified. State and regional directors of the Arts project joined to protest the colonel's military and destructive policy.

The colonel's regime was about a month old when Ellen Woodward called the four national directors to her office to present briefs of their projects. David Niles was also at that meeting; he spoke of loyalty and cooperation, saying that they might be questioned by the House Patents Committee. Turning to the subject of what he called "minor irritations," Niles aimed to make sure that the directors would speak favorably of the WPA administration. The following dialogue is from *Arena:*

"What will you say, Hallie," Niles asked, "if they ask you whether there is censorship in California?"

"Obviously—there's censorship."

"But cancelling *Judgment Day* isn't censorship. It's merely selection."

Act Three

There was a long silence. Then someone asked: "What's *Judgment Day?*"

Flanagan told them that the Elmer Rice play dealt with a court of law in an unspecified totalitarian state, and it showed the depravity, intimidation, and tyranny under dictatorship.

"Well," Henry Alsberg said. He was head of the Writers' Project. "Isn't that the position of our democracy toward dictatorship?"

"It's not a question of the play. That of course is all right," Niles answered. "It's just a matter of selection."

"Who makes the selection?" Flanagan asked. "Isn't the power of selection still vested in the national directors?"

"The whole point is this," said Holger Cahill, director of the Art project. "If the decision as to what music is to be played, what book written, what works of art exhibited, and what plays performed is now to be turned over to state administrators, who know nothing about these matters and hence have a political and not an artistic basis for selection, it is censorship, and if asked we will have to say so."

The four directors, including Nikolai Sokoloff, head of the Music Project, said that if WPA did not approve of their choice of material, it was time to fire them, hire someone else, or openly turn the choice of programs over to the state administrators. But as long as they remained head of the Arts, the four insisted on directing their programs throughout the country.

Niles spoke again of their loyalty and support; they replied that loyalty and support should work both ways. In the meantime, Ellen Woodward had gone out to call Colonel Connolly; when she returned she announced having come to "a complete understanding" with the California administrator. The national directors were to retain artistic control of their programs and personnel, and they could correspond freely with their directors. But *Judgment Day* was only postponed and would take place later.

With this assurance the four national directors, on being questioned before the Patents Committee, said that there was

177

no military censorship of their projects. Flanagan declared that the Federal Theatre probably had been "one of the freest theatres under state and national subsidy in history." Commenting further on censorship, she said that all project heads were censors in a government-supported theatre; part of their duty was to ban material which seemed unsuitable or dangerous for a public theatre.

"We did this constantly on questions of public taste and policy," Flanagan said in her personal history. "But in this matter of selection we were motivated by the general principles of a theatre as vigorous and varied as possible, a theatre belonging . . . to the nation as a whole. We were never actuated by the thought of coming elections, local or national. Any theatre subsidized by public funds which had to concern itself with partisan politics might not end after four years as violently as did the Federal Theatre, but it is probable that long before that it would die of yawning."

ACT FOUR

Ringing Down the Curtain
June 30, 1939

30

"NEW YORK CITY Federal Theatre has almost dropped out of sight," wrote Atkinson in the *Times* on January 26, 1938. That winter the critic followed this up with other statements: "The progressive theatre which Mrs. Flanagan was succeeding into developing is now falling apart. . . . Many believe that she was gracefully pushed to one side because Federal Theatre is unpopular in Washington . . . [where it has] had unpleasant and annoying repercussions. . . . Probably Washington is pleased when it is relatively inactive."

After the Edwards-Kondolf administration had taken over the project for six months, the Supervisors' Council charged that it had only produced a Christmas pageant, *The Advent of the Nativity.* There were three new hits early that year, *Haiti, Prologue to Glory,* and *One-Third of a Nation,* but they had been in rehearsal or were planned when Edwards and Kondolf took over New York in the fall of 1937.

Prologue to Glory, E. P. Conkle's romantic play of young Lincoln, not only got four stars in the *Daily News* but an editorial that praised it as authentic Americana. This was a tribute coming from a paper that was notoriously anti-New Deal. Its critic, Burns Mantle, wrote: "If the Federal Theatre had produced no other single drama, *Prologue to Glory* would doubly justify its history and all its struggles. . . . No citizen of these United States, native or in the making, should be permitted to miss it."

But the newly formed Dies Committee on Un-American Activities regarded *Prologue to Glory* as a propaganda play. J. Parnell Thomas, Republican member of Congress from New Jersey, in a syndicated interview, which was headlined, "Rep. Thomas Bares Red Grip on WPA's Federal Theatre," said, *"Prologue to Glory* deals with Lincoln in his youth and

Your wings are shedding, dearie.
We'll have to requisition another pair.

portrays him battling with politicians. This is simply a propaganda play to prove that all politicians are crooked."

Shortly after that story appeared, Flanagan met Representative Thomas on a train from New York to Washington. She took the occasion to tell him that she was surprised by his statement. He asked her whether she remembered the debate scene in the play. She told him that she did and its subject was, "Resolved that bees are more valuable than men." She also added, as she reports in her memoir, "that Lincoln was really trying, at the time, to discuss the subject of damming up the Sangamon River."

"It seems to me," Flanagan explained, "that the subjects for debate before this forum ought to be alive—subjects of action, useful for living."

"That," said the New Jersey Republican Representative, "is Communist talk."

Thomas was quoted in the *Times* that summer as saying that Federal Theatre was not "only a link in the vast and unparalleled New Deal propaganda machine, but a branch of the Communist Party itself." A man who shared his opinion was Martin Dies, Democratic Representative of Texas, who headed the committee that bore his name. Dies had sworn to get rid of such subversives in the administration as Hopkins, Frances Perkins, Roosevelt's Secretary of Labor, Harold Ickes, Public Works Administration head, and "other Communists and fellow travelers."

That summer of 1938, despite Ellen Woodward's assurance that California was free of bureaucratic control, Flanagan was unable to name a director for the state acceptable to the new administrator. A director had resigned because, with all the paper work, he had no time to function in a theatrical capacity. Flanagan found that to be true herself; the project was becoming more a bureaucratic concern than a producing theatre. Without her approval the state administrator appointed Alexander Leftwich to replace the resigned director. When Flanagan complained to Washington she was told that his appointment had been approved.

Leftwich had a theatre background but he knew nothing

about the project. He announced to the press that his aim was to "get the project on its feet." His first productions were to be *The Gorilla* and *Parlor, Bedroom and Bath.* Within a few weeks he fired all the directors, designers, and technicians; and he closed all current shows, calling it a "housecleaning." Project activity in Los Angeles was stopped, and San Francisco struggled on a bit longer before it, too, came to a halt.

Part of the Federal Theatre's program had been to send out road companies of successes to smaller cities and towns in order to broaden the project's base of public support. Except for a few outstanding hits, this had not been done because Flanagan always met with resistance from some local and state administrator. That summer, in a desperate attempt to win nationwide backing for the project, she proposed a touring plan to Washington. She won Hopkins' support and a nod from President Roosevelt, but Woodward and Niles hesitated to sponsor the plan.

They claimed that it meant crossing state lines and that some state administrators wanted no part of what had become known as a "propagandistic theatre." Flanagan was quick to prove to Washington that of all the plays done by the project only 2 percent could be considered controversial or propaganda for New Deal policies. When Hopkins reaffirmed his support, Woodward and Niles reconsidered and gave permission for a touring program to begin in the fall.

Unfortunately the times were not favorable for such a venture. Federal Theatre was now moving toward retrenchment like other WPA projects. By fall, 1938, the theatre project had left the smart Chanin Building and moved to 1697 Broadway, the modest structure that housed its radio and photographic units. Despite the relief program, the nation was in a deep recession; Republican and Southern Democrats were claiming that the New Deal had been a failure. Though Roosevelt's wages and hours law had managed to win congressional approval, conservatives were determined to trim relief spending and to block further reforms.

That winter Aubrey Williams, a deputy WPA administrator, appeared before the Senate Appropriations Committee for supplementary funds. At the hearing Senator Richard Russell of Georgia accused the theatre project of setting some dangerous precedents by satirizing public figures in its plays, "with funds from the public treasury." Russell was joined by Senator John Townsend, Republican from Delaware, who said that when taxpayers' money was involved, plays had to be careful not to hold people up to ridicule.

Flanagan, who had an instinctive dislike for politicians, could not be bothered about senators who felt they were being ridiculed. The play under question was *One-Third of a Nation,* which she thought was an artistic and social triumph, and a tribute to the power of the theatre as an active force. "Giving apoplexy to people who consider it radical," Jane Mathews quoted Flanagan as saying, "for a government-sponsored theatre to produce plays on subjects vitally concerning the governed is one of the functions of the theatre."

But the Roosevelt administration was forced to look upon it differently. At the time three congressional committees were keeping a watchful eye on all expenditures; and with such criticism in the Senate, the administration feared drastic cuts for the overall WPA program. The politics of relief were thus more important than an expanded theatre project. Rather than face further criticism from conservatives, Washington decided in the end not to let Flanagan have the nationwide tour.

There was another reason for calling off the tour. When the commercial Broadway theatre learned of it, some producers, including Brock Pemberton, raised a howl that could be heard in Washington. Perhaps, if they could have had "a piece of the show," they might have been in favor of the deal; but they saw it as only benefiting the Shuberts, whose chain of theatres would house the project attractions.

The Broadway producers, with little encouragement from the film industry in this case, let out the old cry of "encroachment" for another reason. During the first two years of the project, it had been restricted to advertising shows in the "abc" theatre columns only on Mondays. Federal Theatre had recently secured permission from the League of New York Theatres to advertise them three days a week, but not in the "display" advertising space.

That fall and winter of 1938, as Flanagan spent more time on bureaucracy than theatre, more time defending the project than on producing shows, she faced the struggle to hold on to her reputation as a loyal American, a theatre director and producer, and what remained of the project. She was being surrounded by enemies, inside and outside of the Federal Theatre: superpatriots, radicals, the commercial theatre, film industry, and the conservative congressmen who had now found a way to get Uncle Sam out of show business.

31

BEFORE *The Lost Colony* closed its season that summer of 1938, I wrote Ted Mauntz, the Federal Theatre information director, and asked whether he could use me. I did not bother Flanagan; she was not only busy with theatre problems but faced an upcoming congressional investigation. I reminded Mauntz that I had been fired with six others that spring, but we had been reinstated. He replied, saying to contact Harry Davis of the press unit, when I got back from North Carolina. On September 2, Davis assigned me to the musical *Sing for Your Supper,* which had been in preparation since the Kondolf takeover.

By the time I reached New York, Congressman J. Parnell Thomas had announced that Federal Theatre and the Writers' Project would be investigated as soon as the House Committee on Un-American Activities opened its hearings. Having "startling evidence" that Federal Theatre was operating "as a branch of the Communist Party," he wanted Flanagan to explain why applicants "had to join the Workers' Alliance, a Communist union, to get a job, and why only plays with Communist leanings were produced by the project." The nation's press carried his alleged charges as bona fide news and played them up in front-page headlines.

Chairman of the House Committee was Martin Dies, a flamboyant Texas Democrat, who aimed to continue making such headlines. In 1931 Dies was elected to Congress on a flag-waving program of isolation. In Washington he joined an informal group jokingly known as the Demagogues Club —possibly one reason why Roosevelt and the New Dealers did not take him seriously at first. Dies announced that his mission was to rid the nation of subversives in government who were "undermining the American system"; and

Thomas, who was later imprisoned for defrauding the United States government, promptly joined him in his crusade "to hunt down Communists and fellow travelers in high places."

To Thomas' charges that the project was dominated by Communists, Flanagan released an immediate and pointed denial. Her act violated WPA rules that only the information officer in Washington could answer any attacks in the press. The policy in government circles at the time was to look upon Dies and his committee as a joke, but Flanagan said that their activities never seemed funny to her. The committee continued issuing slanderous statements without giving her or anyone an opportunity to refute them.

That August Flanagan wrote to Representative Dies asking him to hear the Federal Theatre regional directors. She tried to assure him that the project officials were ready to cooperate with the committee, and to answer charges made by his witnesses which she found "biased, prejudiced, and often completely false." She had this letter approved by David Niles, WPA information officer; Dies replied that he would call her, but for the moment he had "a very heavy schedule of witnesses."

Late that month Dies put witnesses on the stand to support his charges against the Federal Theatre. The inquiry was held in the committee's headquarters on Capitol Hill. His first witness was Hazel Huffman, a former worker in the WPA mail department, who said she had been hired by the New York administrator's office to open and read Flanagan's mail. When her spying activities were discovered, Huffman was dismissed; she now claimed that she represented a project group which Equity officials branded a makeshift dual union. These disclosures made her all the more valuable to the committee, for which she was permitted to testify with immunity from any cross examination.

Huffman charged that Aubrey Williams, a WPA deputy, had permitted "the Communist Workers' Alliance to take control of the project." She then reviewed Flanagan's background, saying that the national director had been known as far back as 1928, when her book *Shifting Scenes* appeared, for her "Communistic sympathies, if not membership." The witness also attacked *Can You Hear Their Voices?* because it had received a "rave review" from the *New Masses.*

The woman went on to accuse Flanagan of putting the theatre project before the needs of human beings. This was followed by a listing of what she called "Communist plays" that were produced by Federal Theatre: *Professor Mamlock, On the Rocks, It Can't Happen Here, Hymn to the Rising Sun, The Cradle Will Rock, Revolt of the Beavers, One-Third of a Nation, Power,* and *Injunction Granted.* Then she closed her testimony by asking the Dies Committee to "clear out the Communists on the Federal Theatre" and to put it in the hands of a "good all-around American interested in obeying the laws."

The next witness was actor William Humphrey who had spoken Earl Browder's lines in *Triple-A Plowed Under.* He had nothing to support the charge of subversion with the project; he was quickly dismissed. And the same was to happen to Francis M. Verdi, whose investigation of the validity of actors' complaints had been rejected as useless by Equity.

Witnesses were now called to support Huffman's charges that Federal Theatre was dominated by Communists in the Workers' Alliance and the City Projects Council. A former stage manager testified that alliance members were given preference when plays were being cast. Another witness said that the alliance and the council produced a dangerous un-American atmosphere on the project. Huffman's husband, then a project community drama coach, testified that Communist propaganda was sold on government property and funds for Loyalist Spain were solicited during working hours.

A blond Viennese-born actress took the stand to tell the committee that she had been asked for a date by a Negro on the project, and that whites and blacks fraternized like Communists for social equality and the mixing of the races. A messenger boy described a memorial service held in Carnegie Hall by Loyalist sympathizers on project time. The hearings went on for two days; and the accusations, checked or refuted by no one, were an incredible mixture of truths, half-truths, lies, rumor, and gossip.

Yet the accusations made big news in the nation's press: WPA FACES PROBE AS "HOTBED" OF REDS; FLANAGAN'S A WPA RED; REDS URGE "MIXED" DATE ACTRESS TELLS DIES PROBERS; REDS CONTROL WPA. Such headlines appeared in all the papers, including the *New York Times.* We, in the press department, were surprised to learn that not a single editorial took issue with the committee to refute this biased and unproved evidence against Flanagan and the project.

"WPA still refused to take the attacks seriously," Flanagan said in *Arena.* "Many people believed that this was because it had decided that the Federal Theatre was a political liability and wanted it to end before [the elections of 1940]. I do not think that the appeasement policy . . . started as early as this. . . . WPA was simply following government tradition that attacks on people in government service are not answered by anyone except heads of departments. It goes on the supposition that if you do not answer an attack, the attack will cease."

As the attacks continued, Flanagan wrote Chairman Dies a second and third letter—and received no reply—telling him that he was jeopardizing the jobs of thousands, and that she wished to explain the good work of the project before the committee. This was followed up by a letter from Emmet Lavery, head of the Play Bureau at the time, saying that he was a Catholic, that he had never allowed a Communist play to be done on Federal Theatre, and that he wished to testify before the committee.

Lavery was a playwright whose Catholic drama *The First Legion* was produced on the project; he was later to write *The Magnificent Yankee* and several Hollywood scripts. When, on September 1, Representative Thomas said in the *Herald Tribune* that "practically every play [produced by the project] was clear unadulterated propaganda," Lavery challenged him to debate the matter on the radio. Thomas did not reply; Lavery was not the kind of witness the committee could use to promote its case against the Federal Theatre.

"I have often been asked why we did not demand to attend the hearings of the committee," Flanagan also said in her memoir. Why did she not "insist that project officials or professional theatre people be examined by the committee. And above all, why we did not bring libel suits against some of these congressmen, including Representative Everett M. Dirksen, Republican of Illinois, who called our productions 'salacious tripe'."

But no American citizen has such rights, according to an Article in the United States Constitution which provides that "for any speech or debate in either house they [Senators and Representatives] shall not be questioned in any other place." Thus a congressional committee can hold public or private hearings, choose its witnesses, cite for contempt those who fail to respond, and may not be compelled to hear people who wish to testify.

This article was explained by Lavery, who was trained as a lawyer before he became a playwright. At any ordinary trial court, the accused can demand to cross-examine witnesses; the accused and his lawyer may call expert witnesses on technical points. A congressman is immune from libel suits for remarks made while pursuing his official duties. Caught between the government's policy of silence and the immunity of congressmen on the Dies Committee, Flanagan could only see disaster for the project.

32

WHILE Flanagan was trying to break through the barriers of silence and immunity to defend herself and the project from the committee's reckless and dangerous charges, the New York City project was having one of its best seasons. Five major successes were on the boards: still playing were *One-Third of a Nation, Prologue to Glory, On the Rocks, Haiti,* and the new-comer, Theodore Pratt's *The Big Blow*— the first important production of the Kondolf and Edwards regime.

This drama of a Florida hurricane was produced under the supervision of Morris Ankrum. Principals in the cast were George Mathews, last seen in *Processional,* and Amelia Romano as a young Florida girl. Romano received such good notices that she was chosen to co-star with Henry Hull, of *Tobacco Road* fame, in a Broadway production of *Plumes in the Dust,* a poetic drama about Edgar Allan Poe and his young bride.

Of the shows in preparation, three which showed promise were Yasha Frank's *Pinocchio* with adult actors and vaude-villians; George Sklar's *Life and Death of an American,* the dramatic biography of a typical American from his birth in 1900 to his death in the thirties; and *Sing for Your Supper,* the topical musical revue produced by Harold Hecht and Robert Sour, which I had been assigned to publicize.

I started by interviewing the producers, writers, composers, and directorial staff. Sour and Hecht shared a small office adjoining Kondolf's on the same floor as the information department. Besides being co-producer, Sour wrote some of the show's lyrics; his early song credits included "Body and Soul." Hecht, who assisted in staging the revue, later joined with Burt Lancaster to form a Hollywood com-

Act Four

pany that was to produce several films starring the former trapeze artist of the Federal Theatre Circus.

Of the seven or eight who contributed music, lyrics, and sketches to *Supper,* a gifted pair stood out: John Latouche and Earl Robinson who were responsible for the words and music of "Ballade of Uncle Sam." It was the finale of the revue; later the song won wide popularity as "Ballad for Americans." I spent a lot of time with the pair. They had to keep the material up to date and take care of cast changes during its long rehearsal period before opening at the Adelphi. We were of the same generation, shared social and political causes, and talked of writing plays and musicals.

Keeping "Ballade" topical was a chore mostly for Latouche; he rewrote verses, got them approved or rejected by Hecht, and passed them on to Robinson to fit them to his music. Latouche was a bright young man from Virginia; he had come to New York with a Columbia scholarship, but soon dropped out. His flair for writing light verse opened up the musical stage world for him. Times were hard; it was his friend Virgil Thomson who steered him to Federal Theatre to practice his talents.

Latouche's first task on the project was to arrange songs for the Caravan Theatre revue, *Melodies on Parade.* While I was working with him on *Supper,* Latouche was dating Theodora Griffis, a society girl he was to marry. She was the daughter of Stanton Griffis, a financier who was on the board of Paramount Pictures and Madison Square Garden. Latouche lunched with me at the Automat on 23rd Street; he dined at "21" with Theodora—no doubt her father picked up the check.

After Federal Theatre, Latouche went on to Broadway success. He wrote the lyrics for Vernon Duke's music in *Cabin in the Sky,* starring Ethel Waters, Todd Duncan, Dooley Wilson, and Katherine Dunham. This was followed by the opera, *The Ballad of Baby Doe,* which was done by the New York City Opera company. Latouche also was the author of *The Golden Apple* and wrote lyrics for the musical version of *Candide.*

193

Uncle Sam Presents

I remembered Earl Robinson from *Processional,* for which he composed the incidental music. During the *Supper* rehearsals he was also writing the score with Alex North for *Life and Death of an American.* Robinson, a wonder-boy composer from the West, graduated from the University of Washington with a music degree. He came to New York with straw in his blond hair and a fresh musical talent.

Before joining Federal Theatre, Robinson worked with Harold Rome in 1936, shaping up *Pins and Needles,* the labor musical, which was to bring Broadway fame to Rome. That year Robinson wrote two of his most durable songs, "Joe Hill" and "Abe Lincoln." During the uproar over project cuts in 1937, Robinson was involved with a satiric revue, *Pink Slips on Parade,* which was presented with project actors for a series of benefits.

Along with his friends, Pete Seeger, Josh White, Will Geer, Leadbelly, and Woody Guthrie, Robinson had specialized in folk and workers' songs. He was one of the founders of the "Almanacs," a group which sang at antiwar rallies, union meetings, protests and demonstrations. Later, some Almanac singers banded together and formed the popular "Weavers."

At the *Supper* rehearsals I met Hedley Gordon Graham, whose job was to stage the musical numbers. One of the project's most versatile directors, Graham had staged *O Say Can You Sing* in Chicago, *Altars of Steel* in Atlanta, and the Living Newspapers in New York. The choreography and ensembles were staged by Anna Sokolow, youngest of the project choreographers; when I interviewed her in Greenwich Village for this memoir, she could not remember having been on the show or the project.

Supper became a kind of "talent pool" where actors, singers, and dancers were sent when their shows folded. They were cast in a skit or musical number but, in case of a name performer, new material was sometimes especially prepared. As it happened in many cases, after the performer had rehearsed the number, he either left for a Broadway show or was pulled out for a more important role in another production. In a way this accounted for some of the extended

194

rehearsal period of the show, which brought cries of waste and extravagance from enemies of the project. The *Bassa Moona* group, remnants of the drummers and musicians in *Macbeth,* rehearsed for months in *Supper;* then they were taken out and featured as a Wild African troupe in the Federal Theatre Circus.

Some performers landed in Broadway shows while rehearsing in *Supper.* Eric Brotherson, the first singer to rehearse the "Ballade of Uncle Sam," left for the musical *Beat the Devil,* starring Jack Buchanan. Dan Dailey, Jr., who did song and dance numbers with Virginia Bolen, was engaged to appear with Ethel Merman and Jimmy Durante in *Stars in Your Eyes.* The young dancer Gene Kelly, then unknown, left the cast, and later emerged as the Broadway star of *Pal Joey.*

The form or pattern of *Supper* was simple: Uncle Sam, finding himself with a lot of unemployed actors, singers, and dancers, decides to produce a musical to put them to work and make good use of their talents. This was the basic form of *O Say Can You Sing,* the revue which Kondolf produced with much success as head of the Chicago project. When Flanagan brought him to take over the New York project in late 1937, it was with the purpose of putting together another such revue.

But the similarity between the two revues ends with their form, for the content and spirit of *Supper* was satiric, more topical and social in its significance. It was no doubt somewhat inspired by *Pins and Needles,* the garment workers' revue which ran for three years. While the Chicago show, *O Say,* was lively, boisterous, and brassy, with coarse bits to please a big audience seeking amusement, *Supper* was a topical revue that commented on the pertinent issues and events of the day as well as the lives of those engaged in putting on the show.

After a short prologue between Uncle Sam and a friend, the entire company came on and sang "Sing for Your Supper," which is what they were actually doing. Skits and other numbers followed lampooning the military; Grover Whalen,

Uncle Sam Presents

New York City's official greeter; bored first-nighters in furs and jewels; and even WPA workers in "Leaning on a Shovel," a popular cartoon idea of the times. Show-stoppers such as "Her Pop's a Cop" followed, and a nostalgic recreation of the opening night of *Clorindy* (1900), the first all-Negro musical that was not a minstrel show.

Two of the most popular numbers were "Papa's Got a Job" and the finale, "Ballade of Uncle Sam." The first was a rousing song the company sang on learning that Pop finally got his WPA job; and the ballad closed the show with a spirited reaffirmation of America as the land that fought for freedom and won it for all peoples. The vital young audiences responded to the show and went out the Adelphi singing its message. *Supper* could have played a year or two, but the curtain came down on its sixtieth performance when the project was shut down.

When I recently spoke to Earl Robinson about "Ballad for Americans," I found him to be a serious student of his craft. He was grateful to Federal Theatre for having given him the opportunity to compose for an orchestra, which helped to develop his talent as an all-around musician. Then, speaking about his folk songs, he said, "Of all the cultural forms of entertainment the most spontaneous participation is gained through song. Joe Hill, the poet-song writer of the migratory workers, wrote satiric and militant songs about working people's problems. Songs that are sung in union halls, picket lines, hobo jungles, tramp steamers."

Robinson went on speaking about folk songs—ballads, courting songs, white spirituals, breakdowns from the mountains of Virginia, Kentucky, and the Carolinas—many of which, he said, were handed down from old English, Scotch, and Irish tunes. And songs from the West—Jesse James, Billy the Kid, cowboy work songs, Spanish songs from Texas and New Mexico. Shanty-man songs from the Great Lakes, miners' songs from Pennsylvania, and American Negro songs.

"If you choose a well-known tune, everybody will be interested in your new words for it," Robinson said. "In my own search for lyrics, I came across this excerpt from Abraham

Act Four

Lincoln's first Inaugural Address. With the addition of a single line it became the chorus of my 'Abe Lincoln' song:

"This country with its institutions
Belongs to the people who inhabit it.'
This country with its constitution
Belongs to those who live in it.
'Whenever they shall grow weary
Of the existing government
They can exercise their constitutional
right of amending it,
Or their revolutionary right to dis-
member or overthrow it'."

In spite of its "revolutionary content"—Lincoln's own words— Robinson said that this song has been sung all over the United States, over British noncommercial radio, and by American and British volunteers who fought with the Loyalists in Spain. In 1939, it was sung by a Negro quartet in the zany musical show, *Hellzapoppin'*, starring the comedians Olsen and Johnson.

With the advent of the McCarthy era, Robinson was brought up before the House Committee on Un-American Activities for his "revolutionary songs." This resulted in his being silenced and blacklisted for over a decade. When the committee asked him about his Americanism, Robinson sang his popular, "The House I Live In," a thrilling and folksy tribute to democracy.

33

LATE in August 1938, Federal One officials in Washington directed Paul Edwards to check the employment records of those who had appeared before the Dies Committee. When he sent in his report, Edwards included lists of prominent theatre people who approved of Federal Theatre; letters of endorsement from outstanding public figures who praised the project as an important cultural asset to New York City.

Edwards reported that hostile witnesses were disgruntled employees who had at some time been refused promotion for lack of ability. Hazel Huffman was a typical case: he said that she had brought her husband to his office on many occasions to have him reclassified for a better position. Edwards also reported that Francis Verdi had been dropped because a survey he had made was of no value to Equity or the project.

Regarding the charges that Workers' Alliance controlled the appointment of jobs, Edwards submitted affidavits from employment officials to prove that this was not true. The officials had neither submitted lists of available posts to the Alliance nor consulted it in filling them. Edwards also investigated charges of Communist activities and found they were highly exaggerated, especially since it was illegal to inquire into the political affiliation of anyone engaged on WPA projects.

While WPA officials were silent, despite the denial of charges by the New York administrator, Representative Thomas launched another committee attack, repeating statements that Communists were in control of the project. He now added a new charge: salaries of workers who had testified before the committee had been docked in reprisal.

Flanagan, growing impatient with Washington's silent

policy and hoping to avoid further unfavorable publicity, again wrote Chairman Dies. She once more asked for an opportunity to testify, and also informed him that Thomas' charge of reprisals was false. She explained what we all knew on the project: workers were paid for time spent on the job, but lost time could be made up and pay received for it.

In September we heard Representative Thomas attack Federal Theatre in a radio broadcast, describing it as a "veritable hotbed of un-American activities." He accused Flanagan of having "Communist sympathies," and the plays she chose of destroying "American ideals and suggesting rebellion against the government." This was challenged by Congressman Emmanuel Celler, New York Democrat, who had defended the project at a meeting of the National Theatre Council.

Congressman Celler's reply to Thomas' charges were responsible for reversing WPA's silent policy regarding the committee. It came on the heels of the committee's attack in early September, when witnesses spoke of alleged Communist activities in the New York Writers' Project. Ellen Woodward and other WPA officials now decided to urge the committee to hear evidence from national directors of both projects.

Emmet Lavery and Ted Mauntz, head of our information department, helped Flanagan prepare a defense brief. It was composed of transcripts and production records, lists of plays, sponsors, audience reaction and public testimonials. Flanagan was anxious to face the committee in a public forum, but WPA officials forbade her to refute its charges directly. Finally she was promised a hearing in mid-September.

David Niles and other WPA officials decided however, not to let Flanagan appear before the committee, but chose Ellen Woodward, Federal One administrator, as the person to present briefs of the two projects. On December 5, Woodward did all she could to defend the projects, but was unable to answer specific questions. She did manage to call the committee's method of handling the investigation "un-American," which brought her a reprimand from Representative Joseph Starnes, a member of the committee.

Starnes, an Alabama Democrat in Congress, compelled Woodward to apologize for calling the committee "un-American." Then he lectured her, saying, "You and every other witness are here to answer questions . . . I must insist that you be respectful of this committee . . . We were appointed to ask questions and investigate, not to be investigated." Woodward's favorable testimony was reported, but we noticed that it was treated like a routine item with no headlines.

On December 6, Flanagan was called to testify because the committee wanted more specific information about the theatre project. Hopkins, who was disdainful of Dies and his committee, told Flanagan to "spit" in his eyes. She was sworn in at the hearing by Chairman Dies, whom she described as "a rangy Texan with a cowboy drawl and a big black cigar." Dies, whose obvious intent was to trap her into admitting the project was dominated by Communists, opened by asking about her duties. She bluntly replied: "Since August 29, 1935, I have been combatting un-American activities."

Ignoring her answer or what she had to say about the project's concern for human values, such as returning 2,660 people to private employment, Congressman Starnes now took over and asked about *Shifting Scenes,* the book in which she had praised the Russian theatre. "Was she a member of a Russian organization?" "No," she replied. "Her study of Russian theatre was part of the background of her profession." "Was she a delegate to anything?" Her answer was "no." Like many others she had attended a Russian theatre festival.

Starnes continued, asking whether Communist propaganda had been circulated on the project? "Not to my knowledge," she replied. Were there any orders on her part against such activity? "Yes." Starnes: "Do you believe in the theatre as a weapon?" Flanagan: "I believe the theatre is a great educational force. I think it is an entertainment, I think it is an excitement. I think it may be all things to all men."

Act Four

Starnes quoted from her 1931 article in *Theatre Arts Monthly* about workers' theatres, in which she said, "the theatre is a weapon for teaching class consciousness." Flanagan replied that she had written the article for the magazine as a reportorial assignment.

In her brief Flanagan listed only twenty-six plays out of 924 produced by the project as propagandistic. Starnes asked why she had done them. She tried to make him and the committee understand that propaganda is nothing to fear, that it is nothing but education focused towards a specific goal. The Federal Theatre had done plays propagandizing democracy and freedom and fair labor practices, but certainly not on behalf of Communism.

When Flanagan was asked whether she was in sympathy with Communist doctrines, she said, "I am an American and I believe in American democracy. I believe that the WPA is one great bulwark of that democracy. I believe Federal Theatre is honestly trying in every way to interpret the best interests of the people of this democracy. I am not in sympathy with any other form of government." At another time, she went on record as saying that she was of Scotch-German ancestry, a Congregationalist, and an Independent Democrat.

Chairman Dies took over to ask how many people the project had played to. Flanagan: "25,000,000—a fifth of the population." Starnes returned to the *Theatre Arts* article and read: "They intend to make a social structure without the help of money, and this ambition alone invests their undertaking with a certain Marlowesque madness." He then asked her: "You are quoting from this Marlowe? Is he a Communist?"

"The room rocked with laughter, but I did not laugh," Flanagan reported in her personal history. "Eight thousand people might lose their jobs because a congressional committee had so prejudged us that the classics were 'Communistic'."

Flanagan calmly replied, "I am very sorry. I was quoting from Christopher Marlowe."

201

"Tell us who this Marlowe is," Starnes said, "so we can get the proper reference, because that is all we want to do."

"Put in the record," she replied, "that Marlowe was the greatest dramatist in the period immediately preceding Shakespeare."

When Congressman Starnes regained his composure, he said to his secretary, "Put that in the record because the charge has been made that this article of yours is entirely Communistic, and we want to help you."

We were overjoyed by Hallie's reply and history would not forget Congressman Starnes' blunder: it would end up in his obituary and become the most frequently quoted story in the project's history.

Congressman Thomas took over and spoke about *Revolt of the Beavers.* He asked whether Brooks Atkinson of the *New York Times* had disapproved of it. "Yes," Flanagan replied, "but the *Journal-American* said that it was a pleasing fantasy for children, and a survey by psychologists brought only favorable reaction from children such as 'it teaches us never to be selfish' and 'it is better to be good than bad'."

Representative Harold Mosier, Ohio Republican, returned to the subject of propaganda. He asked whether the project had produced anti-fascist plays? Flanagan replied that some thought Shaw's *On the Rocks* was anti-fascist while others called it anti-Communistic. She added that Shakespeare's *Coriolanus* baffled audiences the same way, saying that "we never do a play because it holds any political bias. We do a play because we believe it is a good play, a strong play. . . ."

Chairman Dies interrupted to ask Flanagan her primary purpose in producing plays—entertainment or education? Flanagan: "The basis for the choice of plays is that any theatre supported by Federal funds should do no plays of a subversive or cheap, or vulgar, or outworn, or imitative nature, but only such plays as the government could stand behind in a program which is national in scope, regional in emphasis, and democratic in American attitude."

"Do you think that the Federal Theatre," asked Chairman

Act Four

Dies, "should be used for the purpose of conveying ideas along social, economic, or political lines?"

"I would hesitate on the political."

Dies then asked her to name one Federal Theatre play, dealing with social questions, where "organized labor does not have the better of the other fellow?" Flanagan mentioned five; he ignored them and asked whether *Power* did not imply that public ownership of utilities was a good thing? And was it proper for a government theatre to take one side of a controversy? Flanagan replied that plays were never chosen to take sides in a controversy.

When Dies announced adjournment for an hour, Flanagan asked, "Do I understand that this concludes my testimony?"

"We will see about it after lunch."

"I would like to make a final statement, if I may."

"We will see about it after lunch," Dies repeated and his gavel fell.

As the session broke up, Representative Thomas, appearing pleased, said to her, "You don't look like a Communist, Mrs. Flanagan. You look like a Republican!"

"If the committee isn't convinced that neither I nor Federal Theatre is Communistic," she said, "I want to come back this afternoon."

"We don't want you back," Thomas said in a laughing tone. "You're a tough witness, and we're all worn out."

Flanagan was not satisfied with the hearing, nor was Ellen Woodward. They told the secretary of the committee that she had not finished her statement. The secretary took the brief, which Flanagan wanted included in the transcript, and tried to assure her that it would be printed. But the brief was not included, nor was it printed. Flanagan mentioned it to David Niles, but nothing more came of it.

The Dies Committee report, filed with the House of Representatives on January 3, 1939, condensed six months of charges against the Federal Theatre project into a short paragraph: "We are convinced that a rather large number of the employees on the Federal Theatre project are either members of the Communist Party or are sympathetic with the

Communist Party. It is also clear that certain employees felt under compulsion to join the Workers' Alliance in order to retain their jobs."

The investigation doomed the Federal Theatre and helped to establish the House Un-American Activities Committee as an institution in Congress. "The mentality of the committee," wrote Eric Bentley in his book *Thirty Years of Treason,* "is as old as persecution itself. Certainly as old as the thirties and forties when the lady (Hazel Huffman) who denounced Hallie Flanagan as a virtual Communist was rewarded for her pains by being hired as an investigator."

34

THE fall and winter that the Dies Committee investigated the Federal Theatre, there was little hope on any front, at home or abroad. While President Roosevelt battled the congressional coalition that aimed to strip New Deal victories and trim upcoming WPA appropriations, England and France negotiated a deal with Hitler and Mussolini at Munich that doomed Czechoslovakia, Austria, and Loyalist Spain, leaving Europe vulnerable to the Führer's blitzkrieg.

During the pact negotiations, Loyalist Spain announced at the League of Nations that it was sending home all international volunteers so that Hitler and Mussolini could withdraw their legions, and leave the Spaniards to fight their war. But with the capitulations at Munich, Hitler was in a position to rush fresh troops and supplies to insure Franco a quick victory. The Loyalists were doomed. On March 27, 1939, Madrid fell; on April 1, Franco announced, "Today . . . the war is ended."

To pacify the conservative coalition in Congress, FDR removed the controversial Hopkins as WPA boss and appointed him as his Secretary of Commerce. The lanky administrator was replaced by Colonel Francis Harrington, a retired Army engineer who, for four years, had directed the WPA manual program. We were fortunate that he was not dictatorial or ambitious like Connolly or Somervell, and was more interested in a soft job than the Arts.

January 1939, Edwards announced additional cuts and asked heads of Federal Theatre units for lists of workers to be given pink slips. Ted Mauntz was one of the half-dozen supervisors who resigned rather than submit such a list. He was replaced by Bernard Simon, a highly-respected Broadway publicist, who later helped me become a member of the theatrical press agents' union. I saw Simon shortly before his death; in response to my query about his job, "Bunny" said that he honestly believed that he had been brought in by Edwards "to act as hatchet man" for the department.

When Congress met that January, with the aim of winning control over expenditures, it heard a report of alleged WPA political activities during the fall elections. Within two days of this report—and that of the Dies Committee on the Federal Theatre—Roosevelt requested a supplemental appropriation. Representative Clifton A. Woodrum, a Virginia Democrat and chairman of the House sub-Committee on Appropriations, demanded a substantial cut in the request.

At the same time we noticed that Woodrum led the attack in the House on the alleged WPA political activities. Taking a cue from the House, a Senate committee questioned Hopkins about them as they were alleged to have taken place during his administration. These congressional acts were interpreted by the press as a rebellion against the administration and predictions appeared about impending funding cuts.

With the growing popularity of their economy moves, the conservatives tagged the Arts projects "frilly and unnecessary," and urged that they be eliminated. Discussing the new conservative upsurge with my project friends Chavkin and Hughes, we agreed that their money-saving gesture was part of an all-out drive to dismantle WPA and other relief projects. This was confirmed when, a bit later, Senator James P. Byrnes, South Carolina Democrat, proposed that all relief programs be combined under a Department of Public Works —making no provision for Federal One to continue.

When Flanagan and other directors brought this proposal to Colonel Harrington's attention, he advised Senator Byrnes that it was a serious omission. The senator demanded to know the real value of the Arts projects, and whether the Federal Theatre was not competing with private enterprise by sending its Chicago company of the successful *The Swing Mikado* to New York, and being responsible for the closing of the D'Oyly Carte company from England. Harrington replied that the famous Gilbert and Sullivan group had come for a limited engagement.

The Swing Mikado broke all records in the history of Chicago's Great Northern Theatre. Since opening in September it had won nationwide acclaim. Sales of Gilbert and Sullivan recordings soared, and nightclub floor shows bloomed like spring flowers. Several producers approached Flanagan with offers to take over the show, but none would guarantee to retain the company intact. John McGee, who had staged it with Harry Minturn, asked permission to present it independently as Houseman and Welles had done with *Cradle.*

Hallie agreed. After all, the project's aim was to return people to private enterprise. But Washington officials disagreed; because of their objections, McGee quit the project—another important loss for Flanagan. Other offers came from such showmen as Mike Todd, the flamboyant Chicago producer; Bernard Ulric and Marvin Ericson, also of Chicago; and Erik Charell, sponsor of lavish Broadway musicals.

Minturn, the Chicago project director, was skeptical of any deal because, if the show flopped, the actors would be back on relief without a job. Flanagan felt his attitude was contrary to WPA policy of making every effort to get people off the project payroll. Though *Mikado* was a prestige show that was making money for Federal Theatre, Hallie was ready to release it to a producer who offered the best deal for the acting company.

In January Ellen Woodward was named to the Social Security Board and was replaced by Florence Kerr, WPA regional head. Kerr and Howard O. Hunter, the new deputy WPA head, were from the Chicago area. As they felt what Hallie called "a pardonable pride in the show which had originated in the territory from which they had come," the pair moved *Mikado* to New York. They ignored previously existing WPA procedure and arranged for a gala premiere more elaborate than had been customary on the project.

Attending the premiere were Eleanor Roosevelt, Mayor LaGuardia, Harry Hopkins, Colonel Harrington, Paul Edwards, Kerr, and Hunter. I watched the radio crew that was preparing for the nationwide broadcast of the event. Flanagan was in San Francisco; she listened to the radio backstage at *Run, Little Chillun,* then in its tenth month, and was happy that *Mikado* was still a project show.

The Swing Mikado repeated its success in New York. Before the musical was moved there from Chicago, Mike Todd had raised the cry of government "competition" and prepared his own version, *The Hot Mikado,* for Broadway. Proud of his reputation as the most ruthless producer of the time, Todd is reported to have spent a week at the Great Northern with members of his staff copying bits of dialogue in shorthand and lifting whatever production ideas they could use.

Todd's version belonged to that class of musicals which he referred to as "meat and potatoes," and Billy Rose, his Broadway counterpart, as "satin and lumber." With Bill Robinson as its star, *The Hot Mikado* was lavishly decorated by Nat Karson who had done the sets and costumes for the project's *Macbeth* in Harlem. Todd also had his director and manager attend the New York opening of *The Swing Mikado* as if to call attention to his upcoming production. The two Mikados inspired a parody on Broadway: "The Red Mikado," a new number in *Pins and Needles,* the Labor Stage musical revue success at the small Princess Theatre.

After a few months on Broadway, the project *Mikado* was turned over to the Chicago producers, Ulric and Ericson. They gave it a new and more expensive production and opened it on West 44th Street at a $2.20 top. Though Todd's version was scaled higher, Bill Robinson was a big draw. *The Swing Mikado* suffered; June saw it back in Chicago for a return engagement.

Though *Variety* surprised us all by stating that Mike Todd was openly *competing with Federal Theatre,* Representative Woodrum in mid-March said before the House Committee on Appropriations that the project was competing with private enterprise. He also said that Federal Theatre did not belong in show business "in open competition with the theatre industry which, at its best, was languishing and sick."

35

ONE of the Federal Theatre's most implacable enemies was Representative Woodrum, whose announced aim was to get Uncle Sam out of show business. As chairman of the powerful House Appropriations Committee, his task in the spring of 1939 was to investigate the Arts projects with a spotlight on the Federal Theatre.

Congressman Woodrum proceded with his inquiry despite President Roosevelt's message to Congress that these white-collar projects had been set up to meet the specific needs of professional workers. Flanagan immediately wrote Woodrum that she was available for a thorough investigation, but like Dies he failed to reply, and we suspected he was playing the same game.

The same witnesses turned up with the same kind of testimony as that before the Dies Committee, but with a slight difference. The Woodrum Committee also used paid investigators. One of them, H. R. Burton, did a three weeks' job on the Arts projects in New York that would have taken a year. Burton in his report mixed fact with fiction regarding *Sing for Your Supper*. It had finally opened April 15 to good reviews and was playing to capacity audiences. I met Burton snooping at the Adelphi; his credentials for the job included a stint as an attorney for the Daughters of the American Confederacy.

Burton reported on such matters as the Adelphi rent; that *Supper* had rehearsed sixteen months and was a big "flop"; Negroes and whites were "mixed and danced together." Woodrum, a southerner, was quick to note the racial character of the revue and other project shows. Burton also reported that *Supper* had "lewd" lines. He gave an example using the word "sexual", which I personally found more innocuous than obscene in the musical number.

While Burton was telling Woodrum that fifty-two out of seventy-nine project workers were members of the Workers' Alliance, another investigator examined the Chicago project. Old actors there complained of favoritism to young people, whom they claimed were getting experience on the project. The committee heard a list of plays the project had produced with such "suggestive and salacious" titles as *The Bishop Misbehaves, Love 'Em and Leave 'Em, Lend Me Your Husband,* and *Up in Mabel's Room.* This was presented as proof of the "vulgar and villainous activities which the people of the U.S.A. were taxed for."

The Woodrum Committee also wanted to know about box-office receipts—whether or not the project was supposed to make money? No one attended the hearings to inform the committee that Federal Theatre had been set up to put jobless people to work—not to make money. Yet, it was at Flanagan's insistence that the project had started charging admissions in January 1936, so that now one hundred percent of production costs—all but salaries—were paid out of box-office receipts.

Witnesses again spoke of Communists as though the project were infested with them. I honestly cannot say that during my two years I knew more than a half-dozen, and I had no way of knowing whether they were members of the Communist Party. It was all hearsay and gossip. Yet no one— neither Flanagan nor Edwards—was present to explain to the committee that it was asking for information which did not exist. We knew that Republican congressmen had made it illegal to obtain such information—political or religious affiliation—fearing that Democrats might be prejudiced against Republicans when seeking relief jobs.

At Burton's suggestion, Charles St. Bernard Dinsmore Walton, a New York project stage manager who had testified before the Dies Committee, told the Woodrum Committee that he had knowledge of "subversive influence" in Federal Theatre. Representative Clarence Cannon, Missouri Democrat and member on the committee, reminded Walton that Mayor LaGuardia had issued an "unqualified statement" that there was no subversive control of WPA in New York City. When Cannon asked Walton to prove his charges, Chairman Woodrum broke in to cut off cross-examination.

"This is no kangaroo court," Cannon said to the Chairman. "I insist that the witness give proof."

"This is my opinion," Walton finally said. "I know Communism when I see it."

During the course of his testimony, Walton told the committee that he had been demoted by his supervisor because he had testified against the project before the Dies Committee.

"Here is a man with a grouch," Representative Cannon said. "All he says is this man said this and that. What is the fact? That's what I want to know."

Then to support his statement of knowing Communism when he saw it, Walton said that he had noticed an audience hissing a policeman in the project drama, *Life and Death of an American.*

"So because in a play an audience hisses a policeman, you think that is sowing the seeds of Communism?" Cannon asked. "If that is sowing the seeds of Communism, then we have Communism all over the country. Cite some play, read us a passage, or give us some specific instance that the project intended to disseminate Communism. You made a very emphatic statement. Now give us some proof of it."

"That is my general observation."

"Sure. But based on what?"

"Based on my knowledge of the theatre and drama."

"Your knowledge of theatre and drama does not qualify you to say that the United States government is deliberately supporting actors disseminating Communism."

"I did not say that either."

"Then give us some testimony on which you base such a conclusion."

"I was asked what information I had," Walton said, "and my opinion, and I gave it."

"That opinion is wholly worthless unless it is supported by

some facts," Cannon said. "The gentleman does not cite a single thing to support such an astounding statement."

That kind of testimony formed the basis for the case against Federal Theatre before the Woodrum Committee: biased and hearsay testimony, as before the Dies Committee. It seemed to me there was a conspiracy between Congress and the press to kill the project. Not a word of Representative Cannon's favorable testimony appeared in the papers, and rarely anything at the time that spoke of its work and achievements. But all the slanderous charges against it were blown up into headlines—as with the Dies group—even if it was stale news.

Flanagan was told by Washington officials that she was not to testify before the Woodrum Committee. The project would be represented by Colonel Harrington and by Paul Edwards. It was unfortunate that Flanagan had been unable to see or brief him on the nature and scope of Federal Theatre.

The colonel spent most of his time telling the Woodrum Committee in a general way about the importance of the Arts projects in American life. When he spoke of Federal Theatre, he admitted that mistakes had been made in administering them, and he promised the committee that he would make drastic changes by reorganizing the project and transferring its directors to Washington so that they could be under close supervision. He closed by saying that he hoped new legislation would not destroy the project. Then Edwards defended us by repudiating charges made before the committee and elsewhere of waste, inefficiency, and Communism.

While Brooks Atkinson defended Federal Theatre in the *Times,* investigator Burton was again called before the Woodrum Committee to repeat his charges. Then, early in June, the eight New York dailies broke a sensational story: "WPA Witness Says Soviets Trained Him in Street Fighting." This tale was based on testimony given by two former Dies witnesses concerning the investigation of the Writers' Project. The testimony, which called the Workers' Alliance a "nursery" for the Communist Party, was cross-examined with no success by Representative Cannon.

Act Four

At the same time a headline appeared in the Washington *Post:* "WPA Theatre May Be Abolished," as Woodrum was telling reporters that two-thirds of Federal Theatre workers had no right to relief, but were on the project because of their membership in the Workers' Alliance. Edwards took issue with this statement, saying that only a few were members of the Alliance and, despite their militancy, its influence was no greater than any of the twenty-nine unions with which the project had to deal in order to produce shows.

But Chairman Woodrum and most of his committee cared no more for Edwards' statements than for those of Colonel Harrington or Representative Cannon. Woodrum and his committee moved swiftly to sponsor a congressional bill that would cut off funds for the continuation of Federal Theatre.

36

As the House Appropriations Committee prepared its bill to kill Federal Theatre, the New York City project was still in full swing. Yasha Frank's *Pinocchio* had been playing to full houses since Christmas. It was broadcast over a nation-wide hookup and was chosen as the first children's play for television. *Life and Death of An American,* with Arthur Kennedy in the title role, was attracting serious attention. *Sing for Your Supper,* attacked in committee hearings and later on the congressional floor, was cheered nightly at the Adelphi as the company sang its rousing finale, "Ballade of Uncle Sam."

Though I was still on the project for the premiere of *Supper,* I left shortly to answer Paul Green's call to handle *The Lost Colony* for another season. I prepared a report on what was in the works and gave it with all my background material to Harry Davis of the press department. Before I reported to Roanoke Island, North Carolina, I worked in the city on the preliminary national campaign with syndicates, magazines, and radio. While on the island, my friend Jim Hughes and the newspapers kept me informed of what was happening on Federal Theatre in New York and Washington.

The project was busy with production plans for the upcoming World's Fair in New York. It announced as the opener Shaw's *Androcles and the Lion,* with an all-Negro cast, which had a long run at the Lafayette. This was to be followed by the four-star hit *Prologue to Glory,* and the mario-nette show winner *Death Takes to the Wheel* on the subject of safe driving, along with a children's play and a dance program. A regular schedule of spot bookings was being played by the Suitcase Theatre, while five Caravan Theatres rolled through the boroughs with plays and musicals.

Act Four

One June afternoon Hallie was checking a Suitcase Theatre performance when a unit manager handed her a newspaper. Its front page carried a story that the House Appropriations Committee, in reporting on the $1,775,000,000 bill for relief funds to the House, included a ban against any of them for Federal Theatre.

"They can't do that, can they?" the manager asked with surprise.

Flanagan soon learned other details of how the bill would affect the Arts projects. Though FDR was granted the amount he had requested for WPA, the funds were subject to several restrictions: the post of WPA administrator would be replaced by a three-man board; workers would receive less than prevailing wage rates; relief personnel on projects for eighteen months or more would be dismissed; the Arts would continue only if sponsored locally; and Federal Theatre would be abolished.

Hallie called Washington. Florence Kerr was out of town. Her assistant Lawrence Morris also was away. (When I recently spoke with Morris, he told me that he had never been told of Flanagan's call.) She then reached Howard Hunter, the WPA deputy, and asked whether the statement was true.

"Yes," he replied.

"Was any reason given in the report for such drastic action?"

"No. Not at all."

Flanagan asked whether Hunter would see her. He agreed and she left immediately for Washington.

"Who's in charge of the fight to save Federal Theatre?" she asked upon reaching his office.

Since they were both good friends of Hopkins, Hunter decided to tell her the truth. "Hallie, there's not going to be a fight for Federal Theatre."

Flanagan was speechless. She knew that WPA officials were in a tough spot; they had to push through a large appropriation or millions of people would be out of work on July 1. She calmly reasoned in *Arena* that opponents of WPA had to be placated to vote it the necessary funds. "These oppo-

215

nents were out to hang the New Deal. Perhaps a hanging in effigy would do. Federal Theatre was ideal for the purpose: although small, it was potent enough to allow the opponents of WPA to trumpet a victory through the press. . . . There are implicit as well as explicit moves in politics as in chess."

From that moment Hallie began a fight for Federal Theatre as she had never fought during its most chaotic days. Now deserted by WPA, she ignored all the red tape that went with it. This was a time for swift and direct action. Had someone told her sooner that no fight would be made, she might have won—or, at least, that is what she believed. She now started a heroic and desperate fight that aroused Washington, Congress, Broadway, and Hollywood to join in her life-and-death attempt to save the Federal Theatre.

Her chances were slim to defeat Representative Woodrum, a shrewd politician who knew that the conservative trend was on his side. But he had gone too far when he told Congress that Federal Theatre had produced nothing of merit. Jane Mathews reports his famous challenge to the project: "Every theatrical critic of any note expressed his disapproval of the project. . . . I have here the manuscript of *Sing for Your Supper.* If there is a line in it that contributes to the cultural life of America, I will eat the whole manuscript. . . . It has been a complete flop and it cost over $300,000 to produce. So we are going out of the theatre business."

Flanagan contacted friendly congressmen and the New York drama critics. Within a few days she reached more than a dozen members of the House, including Emmanuel Celler, John J. Dempsey, Vito Marcantonio, who all promised to defend Federal Theatre; and Representative Mary Norton would introduce an amendment in the House restoring the project in the Appropriations bill.

Though Woodrum was said to hate the theatre, he was badly misinformed to say that "every drama critic of note expressed his disapproval" of Federal Theatre. During a debate in the House, Representative Marcantonio responded by reading a telegram in its defense signed by a dozen New York critics, including Atkinson, *Times;* Mantle, *Daily News;*

Act Four

Sidney Whipple, *World-Telegram;* Wolcott Gibbs, *New Yorker;* Otis Ferguson, *New Republic;* Allene Talmey, *Vogue;* Paul Peters, *Life;* Joseph Wood Krutch, *The Nation;* Euphemia Wyatt, *Catholic World;* Kelcey Allen, *Women's Wear;* and Arthur Pollock, Brooklyn *Eagle.*

"If a fair and impartial estimate of the work of the theatre project had been wanted," the critics' telegram read, "we should have been glad to give him [Chairman Woodrum] our opinion for what it is worth—in consensus, that the theatre project of New York . . . has been on the whole an institution of great value to the life of the community and that apart from its Broadway productions it has performed many less conspicuous services whose value could not be estimated. We believe emphatically that the project should not be abolished."

Representative Adolph Sabath read into the *Congressional Record* Atkinson's *Times* article of May 28, in which the critic said, "Being the most conspicuous of the WPA Arts projects, Federal Theatre is the one Congress enjoys worrying most. Art seems like boondoggling to a congressman who is looking for a club with which to belabor the administration and there is always something in Federal Theatre that can be blown up into a scandal. But for socially useful achievement, it would be hard . . . to beat the Federal Theatre, which has brought art and ideas within the range of millions of people all over the country and proved that the potential theatre audience is inexhaustible. . . . It has been the best friend the theatre as an institution has ever had in this country. . . . It deserves to be rescued from partisan politics which, on one hand are creeping into its administration, and on the other are threatening to put it out of business."

The night of June 14, Hallie sat in the gallery of the House of Representatives and "watched a scene which, if dramatized on one of our stages, would have resulted in a charge that we were libeling the legislative branch of the United States," she wrote in her memoir. "Every mention of a so-called salacious title—any title with the word love—was

217

greeted with howls and catcalls." And the calm voice of Representative Celler, who spoke for the project, was "shouted down."

The plays attacked had been listed in a release, "WPA Foibles," issued by the Republican National Committee Publicity Division, Washington, D.C. To quote from it: "Could any more suggestive and salacious titles be found for plays on parade before the American public? Are the people of this country to be taxed to support such vulgar and villainous activities?" The plays listed included Clemence Dane's *Bill of Divorcement* and Susan Glaspell's early Pronvincetown success, *Suppressed Desires,* along with several Broadway hits.

Representative Mary Norton rose and faced a hostile House to say, "I do not believe anything that anyone can say tonight is going to change the temper of this House, but I beg you before proceding with this bill to stop and consider what you are doing to 5,000 men and women on this project." She denied charges of Communism, mentioned the support of churches, and then added: "I have heard employers of labor criticized on the floor of the House, but I venture to say that the most cold-blooded employer would hesitate to discharge his employees with no notice whatsoever. . . . This is the sort of thing responsible for Communism."

She too was shouted down. One of the loudest voices was that of Representative Everett Dirksen, Illinois Republican, who hated the New Deal. He ran down the list of plays, saying, "If you want this kind of salacious tripe, very well vote for it [Norton Amendment], but if anybody has any interest in the real cultural values you will not find it in this kind of junk, and I suggest that we have the bill as it is and vote down the amendment."

The hour was past midnight, the temperature was ninety-six degrees; members of the House perspired, their tempers were higher than usual. As Flanagan sweated it out in the gallery, she could see that the House was in no mood to debate the question. With no further word on the Norton Amendment, Representative William Bankhead, Speaker of the House, pounded his gavel and someone called for the vote. The Amendment lost 56 to 192. Then after 1 A.M., in the longest House session of the year, the weary representatives voted 373 to 21 to accept the Appropriations Committee Relief bill that doomed Federal Theatre.

Flanagan still thought she had a chance to save the project in the Senate. She and a staff studied the list of senators for names and sympathizers. She sent them reviews, reports, and telephoned them. She called Equity and other theatrical unions to send telegrams, prepared petitions for actors to get signatures in Times Square, and stirred up theatre people from Broadway to Hollywood to help rescue the project from its prejudiced and, in most cases, uninformed congressmen.

Her last-minute fight to save the project became a nation-wide crusade. Even the commercial theatre now joined the fight. All the theatrical unions, Equity, IATSE, the four A's, Theatre Arts Committee, League of New York Theatres, the Tri-Guilds of Hollywood, and other unions sent telegrams to congressmen and the White House. Joining the cause were Eddie Cantor, Helen Hayes, Burgess Meredith, Richard Rodgers, George Abbott, Moss Hart, Harold Clurman, and Clifford Odets.

Though I was down on the Carolina coast, I was more involved with the crusade to save Federal Theatre than with the opening of *The Lost Colony.* I felt stranded and exiled— a virtual deserter—when I read Jim Hughes' reports of what everybody was doing for the project. He and our friends had joined dancers and chorus girls in marching up and down Broadway, protesting, and getting signatures for petitions to save it.

I had left with a feeling that the project was doomed, but now my hopes soared for its fight to continue. Federal Theatre would win despite the forces of ignorance, prejudice, and greed, which were lusting for the limelight. Forces that had been set in motion by what Flanagan considered the most backward elements of the nation: "self-appointed defenders of Americanism."

37

FROM coast to coast Flanagan's Federal Theatre crusade was on, involving people in theatre, the arts, and politics. Among those whom Theatre Arts Committee rallied to its side were the biggest Broadway and Hollywood names. The most outspoken was Tallulah Bankhead, daughter of the Speaker of the House, and niece of John Bankhead, the Alabama senator. She embraced it as a personal cause; Herman Shumlin, producer of her then current success, *The Little Foxes,* hailed her as "Federal Theatre's Joan of Arc."

Tallulah (I take the liberty of calling her by the name she loved because I publicized her revival of *Private Lives*) appeared on the Senate floor in mid-June to support the Wagner-Downey-Coffee Amendment. Hughes wrote me that it was a bill to establish a Federal Bureau of Fine Arts—partly to save Federal Theatre during the present crisis. Its sponsors were three Democratic senators and ardent New Dealers: Robert Wagner, New York; Sheridan Downey, California; and Claude Pepper, Florida.

The actress showed up in the Senate with her father, Representative William Bankhead, and her uncle, Senator John Bankhead. They were both Democrats; while her father was a strong New Dealer and in favor of the bill, her uncle had to be convinced of the merits of government subsidy of the arts. When Tallulah saw she could not convert her uncle, a man more interested in the cause of Alabama farmers than in that of the nation's actors, she turned to the committee itself, and urged them not to deprive Federal Theatre workers of the dignity and self-respect due every American.

Flanagan, who was waiting close by at the time, was called in to answer charges made by the House Appropriations Committee. In reply to the accusation that the project was overloaded with nonrelief personnel, she testified that 90 percent of the workers were from relief rolls; that instead of their seeking to make a career of their relief jobs, 2,660 had been returned to private employment—I was one of them—and 80 percent were now members of accredited theatrical unions.

"As the friendly questioning of the senators moved forward, I could see that once more the question of our double identity was at the root of many of our difficulties," Flanagan wrote of that hearing in *Arena.* "Because we were a relief enterprise, people found it difficult to believe that the good acting was turned in by actors in need of relief; because we were also a theatre enterprise, they were impatient with the strange variety of talent which we took from relief rolls."

While the committee discussed the $2,000,000 that Federal Theatre had taken in at the box office, it received a telegram from a Hollywood group, headed by James Cagney, Edward Arnold, and Pat O'Brien. The group was ready to guarantee the production costs of the California project—if the theatre were permitted to continue with the other Arts projects on the basis of local sponsorship.

A large and miscellaneous group rallied to the cause of Federal Theatre. Speaking in a nationwide broadcast were Orson Welles, Jane Cowl, George Jessel, Herman Shumlin, and other Broadway figures. New York critics and columnists Heywood Broun, Leonard Lyons, Walter Winchell, Olin Downes, John Martin, and Eleanor Roosevelt. Tyrone Power flew into Washington from Hollywood to deliver the resolution of the Motion Picture Guild for passage of the Wagner-Downey-Pepper bill.

I learned from Hughes that Broadway expanded its efforts before the committee. Frank Gillmore, head of Equity, and Herman Shumlin, a member of the League of New York Theatres, testified that it was not competing with the commercial theatre. James Brennan, IATSE representative of the stagehands' union, sang its praises. Colonel Harrington repeated the Federal Theatre's accomplishments. Raymond Massey, then starring in Robert E. Sherwood's success *Abe*

Lincoln in Illinois, offered to debate Congressman Woodrum on a network broadcast.

In Hollywood the Motion Picture Guild set up two nation-wide radio programs on behalf of the project. Film stars Claudette Colbert, Melvyn Douglas, Ralph Bellamy, Joan Blondell, Henry Fonda, James Cagney, Dick Powell, Patricia Morrison, and Al Jolson participated in an hour show, "Take It Away, Hollywood!" The other program was "Florida Wheel," a poetic tribute to the state project written by Flanagan, with a plea for the theatre's survival.

Lionel Barrymore spoke on this program, calling himself not only an old actor but a citizen of the United States. "I think it's dangerous for a nation to start proving what a fine country it can be and then . . . let it slide back to the days of the Depression." He said that any cutting of the arts program was "like taking one of the stripes out of the American flag," and asked Congress to remember that "the American people have never let anything be taken away from them—permanently."

The Federation of Arts Union in New York sponsored a broadcast and staged a rally in the Majestic Theatre which was responsible for a new wave of telegrams to Washington from the League of New York Theatres and the American Federation of Radio Artists. The writer Edna Ferber defended the project, also Bishop Francis J. McConnell of the Methodist Episcopal Church.

Mathews quotes Hallie as saying, "We know now that we have a better than a fighting chance in the Senate and a fairly good one in the House after mobilizing this support for the project." On June 26, the Appropriations Committee sent an amended version of the Relief Bill to the House; now the theatre, along with the other Arts projects, was to be continued—if it got local sponsorship. Debate began in the House on the Wagner-Downey-Pepper bill calling for one percent of WPA funds to be earmarked for the Arts projects.

Flanagan at this point felt that all her efforts were amply rewarded. "Such spectacular support had an effect on the proceedings of the Senate where, aside from the almost unbelievable attacks by Senator Robert Reynolds and Senator

Act Four

Rush Holt, consideration of Federal Theatre was just and judicious. It was impressive to see that every senator we had been able to supply with facts not only voted for the amendment reinstating Federal Theatre, but spoke for it." And Senator Bankhead, Tallulah's uncle, was among them.

Senator Reynolds of North Carolina became a super-red-baiter in telling his colleagues that Federal Theatre was controlled by Communists who used plays to spread "the doctrine of Communism at the expense of the American taxpayer." This fact alone was enough for the Senate, he said, "to condemn the project . . . to the ashcan of oblivion."

Commenting on Reynolds' attack, Jane Mathews wrote, "Hopelessly uninformed and irresponsible, Reynolds' red-baiting remarks were thoroughly consistent with his self-appointed role as a defender of Americanism." To a man like Reynolds, Americanism meant the free enterprise system of private utilities, the textile and tobacco industries, which had sponsored him as a senator from North Carolina.

Reynolds' attack did not go unanswered. Senator Pat McCarran, Nevada Democrat, was the first to rise and set the tone for the project's defense. Quoting Roosevelt's memorable words from his first inaugural address, "What we have to fear in America is fear itself," McCarran said that we should be on our guard for fear produced by those who are "forever and always . . . using the bugbear of Communism to scare people in order that they themselves might rise up and thus be held up as champions against the so-called dangers of Communism."

With the information that Flanagan had given the senators, they rallied to its support. Senator Pepper declared that the new bill included a loyalty oath which could check the alleged Communist threat. Senator James Mead of New York bluntly said that he doubted such a threat existed at all. Mead went on to say that, with the majority of employees on the project belonging to established theatrical unions, the number of Workers' Alliance members in the Communist Party was negligible.

Senator James J. Davis, Pennsylvania Republican, who was convinced in 1936 that the project was controlled by radicals, now said that, with the new loyalty oath, Congress was already correcting the problem and there was no further need to throw innocent people out of work.

His turnabout was too much for Senator Reynolds, who had considered Davis an ally in his fight to kill the project. The superpatriot from North Carolina again lashed out, this time quoting the most incriminatory parts of testimony given before the Dies and Woodrum Committees, and closed by making a big issue among the southern senators of the white actress' complaint that she had been asked for a "date" by a Negro on the project.

"The attack reached . . . new depths," wrote Mathews, "with a description of the project's 'unsavory collection of Communistic, un-American doctrines, its assortment of insidious and vicious ideologies,' [its] 'putrid plays . . . spewed from the gutters of the Kremlin,' and advertised on marquees which were, of course, 'red.' Not only was Federal Theatre pro-Communist, the senator asserted, but it was also unprofitable."

While saying that there was "no lady in America of higher character than Mrs. Flanagan," Reynolds insisted that the project needed "someone with old-fashioned commonsense rather than some college professor." Prior to this harangue, Flanagan had telephoned our friend Paul Green, the North Carolina Pulitzer Prize playwright, asking him to attempt to persuade the senator to call off his attack.

A few days later when Green arrived on Roanoke Island for the opening of *The Lost Colony,* he mentioned that Hallie had called him in Chapel Hill and asked him to please intercede with the Carolina senator to halt his attack. Green agreed to telephone Reynolds, but warned her it would do no good. He told me what the senator had said."Knowing Bob Reynolds and his suspicion of anything generous or 'radical', I was sure that no appeal would be worthwhile. But I made the appeal as fervid and fervent as I could, and Reynolds replied with categorical repetitiveness, 'The Federal Theatre is full of Communists and you know it. Come next Thursday it is a dead duck.' And it was."

38

Despite Senator Reynolds' tactics, Federal Theatre still had a chance. Hallie had told me months earlier that if only the project could get a fair hearing, free from the prejudice of radical smears, that people would certainly recognize the value of our efforts. Now Senator Henry Ashurst, the Democratic Chairman of the powerful Judiciary Committee, tried to appeal to the "best" in his colleagues with his ringing "Tiberius" speech in which he argued that only art endures and that in voting against art, the Senate was voting against the very things that are the greatest accomplishments of nations and mankind.

One by one the House changes in the Relief Bill were discarded and hope for Federal Theatre soared again. After a long debate over percentages of appropriations the senators voted overwhelmingly in favor of the bill and we were saved, one day before the deadline ending all WPA projects. We were delighted. Perhaps Hallie was a prophet after all. As she later wrote in *Arena,* "The only time Federal Theatre had a fair hearing upon the issues we won."

But the bill, which would have provided us with only a third of the funds from the previous year, was sent to a conference committee and the House members refused to compromise on their pledge to end Federal Theatre. The whole future of WPA now hung in the balance. Would the jobs of two and a half million workers be sacrificed for a "handful" of theatre people?

Once again compromise ruled. The House members led by the determined Woodrum were prepared to stall the entire WPA budget rather than give in to the continuation of Uncle Sam as a theatrical producer. Tempers rose and fell. Solutions were offered and rejected. Finally, with time running short, the Senate opposition collapsed. After June 30, 1939, in exchange for generous severance pay for those presently employed funds would no longer be available for the Federal Theatre. The reprieve of a few hours earlier now seemed hollow and the whole project appeared doomed.

Woodrum presented the compromise bill to an elated but weary House and demanded that Uncle Sam get out of show business. There was virtually no opposition left. The vote was 321 to 23. Now only the Senate was left to preserve what Hallie had worked so hard to create and sustain.

But the fight was over. In the Senate we were confronted once more with the "red" smears which had haunted the project for so many months. The debate was familiar, hysterical, and rancid. Under the withering accusation of "Communist" everything that we had accomplished was demeaned and belittled. Senator Dirkson's earlier cries of "salaciousness" were repeated by the vitriolic young Rush Holt and all of the unfounded and ignorant Dies committee conclusions were paraded as profound and meaningful.

At ten o'clock that night the WPA bill with the provision excluding Federal Theatre was on Roosevelt's desk. He called the exclusion discriminatory legislation to which he was personally opposed, but he signed.

Hallie refused to give up, but the battle was lost. It was ironic that the death of the project—on a rider which accompanied renewed WPA funds—went unnoticed by many. In *Arena* she reports that one congressman called a few days later to inquire about the project in his state.

"But, Congressman, there is no Federal Theatre. You voted it out of existence."

A stunned silence and then, "What?"

"It was abolished on June 30 by Act of Congress."

Again silence.

Then a shocked and heavy voice said, "Was that the Federal Theatre?"

On Broadway our shows closed. Hughes wrote that at the Maxine Elliott, where *Life and Death of an American* premiered a month earlier, Director Charles Freeman told a stunned audience that Federal Theatre no longer existed. "Quite simply, we have been eliminated."

Act Four

For the final performance of *Pinocchio* at the Ritz, Yasha Frank improvised a new ending. Each night the puppet, having conquered greed and selfishness, became a living boy. But on this last evening the transformation did not take place. Instead, while the cast sang that his life had been too short, Pinocchio, only a piece of wood, died. He was then placed in a pine coffin which bore the dates of his brief life: Born December 23, 1938. Died June 30, 1939.

Without dropping the front curtain the stagehands struck the set. Most of the audience stayed to watch and then followed the cast and crew out of the theatre on an improvised march along 49th Street. This hastily assembled funeral procession bore hand-lettered signs announcing the MURDER OF PINOCCHIO and the DEATH OF FEDERAL THEATRE and attracted sympathizers and curiousity seekers along the way. It was a far cry, Hughes told me, from the spirited and exuberant parades which had been part of the Federal Theatre story. I wondered if any of the exuberant May Day marchers, strike protesters, or *Cradle Will Rock* ticket holders were there for the last silent parade into Duffy Square or for the raggedly sung National Anthem which climaxed their final vigil for Pinocchio.

But my sympathies went out most strongly to the cast and crews of *Sing for Your Supper,* the show that I had publicized, which was still running at the Adelphi. It was fitting that *Supper* be one of the last to close because its biting lyrics and frequently comic innuendos had come to the attention of more than one congressman and committee over the past few months. Production Manager H. Gordon Graham recently told me how the company chose the moment right after the actor playing "Papa" had finally gotten a WPA job to voice their reaction to the demise of the project. After a rousing version of "Papa's Got a Job" the stage filled with actors celebrating the happy event and then suddenly, everything stopped. Graham walked down to the footlights and told the startled audience, "Yes, Papa had a job, but they're taking it away from him at twelve o'clock tonight."

The show resumed and Graham told me than the cast never sang "Ballade" with more fighting spirit than they did that night. As Uncle Sam came on to survey his people and the revue swung into its climax, the stage filled again, this time with the sound of John Latouche's ringing lyric of America, a land of all people, the et ceteras and so forths, who do the work of the country.

The house was silent as though it was catching its breath. Then a young girl with a ribbon in her hair asked Uncle Sam, "Did they all believe in liberty those days?" The answer from the entire company, set to Earl Robinson's marching music, rang out in a dramatic crescendo of the "Ballade of Uncle Sam" which concluded with a chorus of lines from the Declaration of Independence.

Afterwards, audience members lingered in the lobby and in the street outside, uncertain of how to mark the end of the project. Backstage the actors lingered too and then drifted away—unemployed.

39

FEDERAL Theatre came to an end as it had started: with what Hallie Flanagan called "a fearless presentation of problems touching American life." Instead of steering a course which would have kept it "out of the papers," she had approved hundreds of productions—entertaining, educational, provocative—providing they met her standards of good theatre. To her, good theatre could help America become a better country for more people—the ideal of democracy.

From the inception of the project she had to face negative forces that were suspicious of the "adult, free, uncensored theatre" that Harry Hopkins had promised her. With the banning of the first Living Newspapers, she saw that these forces would try to block a theatre program which aimed to educate its vast new audience about the problems of government, politics, relief, fascism, business, housing, labor, power, and the role of the consumer in our changing economic life.

Though serious issues were explored in a small fraction of Federal Theatre productions, she understood why superpatriots and other extremists would not even want a small percentage of Americans to think. These groups were as afraid of thinking people as Southern Democrats were afraid of the project, not because they said it provoked class hatred, but because it spoke of closer relationships between classes and races.

Federal Theatre was perhaps the most conspicuous of the relief projects. It was also the one that Atkinson of the *Times* said congressmen enjoyed annoying most because it was doing something that they could turn into a scandal. The project cost the taxpayer money; it had to deal with unions, old and new; it did not bar aliens, members of minority races, or parties. It was a small but viable example of the New Deal's social aims and ideals, which were considered inimical and radical by extreme elements on both sides of the Mason-Dixon line.

Flanagan blamed Congress for the fate of the project by not changing the regulations that governed it. Congress did change the ruling to bar aliens from all WPA projects; but at the same time it could have extended this regulation to include members of any specific minority party. To quote from her memoir: "Congress punished us for failing to take action which was its exclusive prerogative. It was hardly necessary to tear down the house to get at the mouse in the cellar."

Had she been told earlier that Washington planned no defense of the project, Flanagan could have gotten her crusade rolling sooner, and there would have been a chance to save it. Though she was aware that some of the project's weaknesses, such as its ambiguous work-relief status, were inherent in the WPA setup that gave birth to Federal Theatre, Flanagan conceded that Congress, in giving it life, had the right to end it. Yet she justly lamented that Congress had let itself be misinformed by the prejudiced testimony of two investigating committees; and that the project's fate was eventually doomed by the immunity of its accusers and the bureaucratic silence of the administration.

Flanagan accepted defeat, but she wondered for some time afterwards how it was possible, with such a record of achievements and the incredible support in its last week, that Federal Theatre was killed by Congress. For the project was ended, not as an economy move, but because Congress, despite protests from many of its members, considered it a political issue, not a human or cultural one. She could only conclude that its end was a political gesture by Washington to appease the growing conservative forces against the New Deal's liberal social program.

Federal Theatre's production record proved that Uncle Sam could put on shows and have hits as well as any legitimate producer. It also proved that millions of Americans

Act Four

wanted theatre if it could be brought to towns and cities at a price they could afford to pay. But such a nationwide theatre could not function without government subsidy, Flanagan contended, because its scope was beyond that of private enterprise and commercial motives.

During its short, spectacular life Federal Theatre had as many as 185 producing units in 28 states playing to a combined weekly audience of 500,000. It presented almost one thousand productions before a total audience of 25,000,000—one-fifth of the nation's population at the time. Its largest audiences attended free shows in parks, armories, and public institutions; and its box office admissions of $2,018,775 covered all production expenses except labor. Out of an average personnel of 10,000 during its four years, 2,660 persons were returned to private industry. The entire cost of the project was $46,207,779—a tiny fraction of the total WPA expenditure during those years, or approximately the cost of a battleship in 1940.

For such a sum the Federal Theatre launched the first people's theatre in America, a nationwide Negro Theatre, a theatre for children and for religious drama. It gave opportunities to dramatists, composers, designers, performers, and extended to supervisory and other important posts women. It discovered talent that won fame on Broadway and in Hollywood, introduced the Living Newspaper form, and sponsored the writing of regional and historical drama. It developed in an exploratory way new uses for theatre in education, therapeutics, diagnosis, social, and community drama. Federal Theatre left its mark, as the nation's critics repeatedly said, on the theatre and the entertainment world.

But the project's outstanding achievement was the discovery and development of a nationwide audience. If a government is interested in making its people better citizens and individuals, Flanagan firmly believed that such a government should concern itself more and more with theatre. Not theatre as a luxury but as a social necessity. She believed theatre was "a necessity because in order to make democracy work the people must increasingly participate; they cannot participate unless they understand; and the theatre is one of the greatest mediums of understanding."

Flanagan also believed that "such a theatre is a life force" to combat the negative pressures of ignorance, greed, and prejudice. "Creating for our citizens a medium for free expression such as no other form of government can assure, and offering the people access to the arts and tools of a civilization which they themselves are helping to make, such a theatre is at once an illustration and a bulwark of the democratic form of government," she wrote in *Arena.*

Every decade or so, when the theatre has a box-office low, Broadway showmen lament that the theatre is a "fabulous invalid," which keeps rising from its bed of ashes. During the Depression, George S. Kaufman wrote a sentimental play with that title to show that the theatre would continue to live as long as there were poets with feeling and imagination.

Flanagan went further: she believed that the theatre had "a tremendous power to stir up life and infuse it with fire. . . . It is probable that during [the years 1935–1939] more discussions of the theatre took place . . . than in all the other years of our congressional history put together. . . . A senator who fought for Federal Theatre told me that months after it was ended, fights about its merits and demerits were still going on in congressional cloakrooms. No one fights over a dead art or a dead issue."

Nor does a congressman like Clifton Woodrum, who led the fight to kill the project, say even in jest, "if there is a line or passage in it [*Sing for Your Supper*] that contributed to cultural or educational life of America, I will eat the whole manuscript." Congressman Woodrum got his chance to eat it the summer of 1940 when the musical's finale, renamed "Ballad for Americans," was chosen as the theme song of the Republican National Convention in Philadelphia—a year after he buried the project.

Flanagan had these final words to say in her personal story of the project: "The President of the United States in writing to me of his regret at the closing of Federal Theatre referred to it as 'a pioneering job.' This it was . . . . Its significance lies in its pointing to the future. . . . It was perhaps the triumph as well as the tragedy of our actors that they became the abstract and brief chronicle of the time. . . . The 10,000 anonymous men and women—the et ceteras and the and-so-forths who did the work, the nobodies who were everybody, the somebodies who believed it—their dreams and deeds were not to end. They were the beginning of a people's theatre in a country whose greatest plays are still to come."

40

THE Federal Theatre died because Hallie would not play it safe. It was not her style. Nor was it the style of a lot of people during those troubled and exhilarating times. I remember a speech by Ernest L. Meyer, who wrote a provocative column in the *New York Post,* to the American Newspaper Guild when we were debating whether we should join the CIO or stick with the craft-oriented AFL. "If we don't all hang together," he said, "we'll be hanging separately. And as for jobs, we'll be tying pink ribbons on packages at Macy's."

I believed him. It was a time when things seemed clearer, when the division between friends and enemies was more distinct, and when right and wrong seemed obvious. Who could be opposed to the striking Kentucky miners, the fighting Spanish Loyalists, or those protesting the fascist menace in America? I had no doubts that the Federal Theatre project was under attack for reasons that had little to do with the quality of our productions and as the forces joined for the final assault I realized that Hallie would lose.

That was forty years ago. And now I am tempted to see it differently. After all, it was a time of drastic social upheaval and many of our "enemies" were genuine in their belief that Roosevelt and the New Deal were destroying the very fabric of their lives. And there were those who wanted to burn down everything and begin again.

Forty years ago. . . . We did seem happy in spite of the hardships; in spite of the economic chaos that threatened to wipe out jobs and careers as soon as they were started. It was a time when all I could slip on my bride's finger was a cigar band, but we laughed about it. It was a time of making the best of it, of imagination and daring, of doing what we had not done before, and, if we failed, trying something else with the same vigor and enthusiasm.

But the odor of nostalgia is not always sweet and I have resisted the temptation to "revise" what was happening all around me because of the rush of later events. I spoke to a number of former project heads and others while preparing this memoir and some of them blamed Flanagan more than anyone else for the demise of the project. Though no radical herself, they admitted, she had allied herself with those on the left and was caught in the conservative backlash. But I contend that she could do nothing else. Hallie found the liberals more talented, more imaginative, and more original; more in line with what she thought belonged in a theatre of a changing world—a theatre of "adventure."

Welles and Houseman, Edward Goodman, Morris Watson, Arthur Arent were not Hallie's "fair-haired boys" because of how they voted; she recognized and respected their talent. Had this first venture in government theatre been less alive and less talented, we all knew it might have lived longer. Yet none of us who were a part of it regret that the project from its inception stood against ignorance, fear, and intolerance, all masquerading in the guise of patriotism.

And there were scoundrels. Men and women who were unable or unwilling to distinguish between Stanislavski and Stalin. Congressmen who attacked productions they had never seen and who formed ignorant opinions based upon play titles read into the *Congressional Record*. Small minds who feared Flanagan because she was a woman or a college professor or because she had traveled abroad. The repercussions lasted two decades in the blacklists, the fear of ideas and the harassment of those who criticized the American way of life. Even I, who never joined anything more radical than the Newspaper Guild, was interviewed by two greycoated F.B.I. agents because I was a friend of Haakon Chevalier.

But after thirty years in the theatre, publicizing over a hundred musicals and half as many plays, I can honestly say that the Federal Theatre set a standard that has rarely been equaled or surpassed by the commercial stage. Though I worked on many of the theatre's later hits, *The Voice of the Turtle, South Pacific, Anna Lucasta, One Touch of Venus, Porgy and Bess, Kismet, My Fair Lady,* and others, the only ones that linger in my memory are *Lady in the Dark, The Visit, Long Day's Journey Into Night, Porgy and Bess,* and *My Fair Lady.*

But when it comes to the Federal Theatre, I must mention the four Living Newspapers, *Triple-A Plowed Under, One-Third of a Nation, Injunction Granted,* and *Power.* Then the Harlem *Macbeth* and the magical *Doctor Faustus.* The delightful *Revolt of the Beavers.* The Yiddish folk musical *We Live and Laugh* down on the Lower East Side. Tamiris and her dance drama, *How Long Brethren? Prologue to Glory,* about the young Lincoln. And the timely productions of *Class of '29, It Can't Happen Here,* and the runaway, *The Cradle Will Rock. Sing for Your Supper* for its fresh, imaginative and youthful spirit; and its "Ballade of Uncle Sam," which Martin Dies, in his efforts to destroy the project, described as "an American version of the 'Internationale'."

I would like to think that Federal Theatre left its mark on the commercial theatre as it did on me, but I cannot say that it has. From what I have seen I can safely say that for all its novelty, extravagance, and popularity, today's theatre, on or off Broadway, strikes me as spirited in body and light in the head; it is imitative, nostaligic, inflated, and ingenuous in its aim to amuse, entertain, and shock a new affluent audience. Using techniques of big business, the theatre like the big art shows has become a profitable "cultural" commodity.

But more discouraging is the fact that those latter-day Federal experiments in the theatre—those National Endowments and CETA projects—seem obsessed with popularity and publicity rather than talent. "Elitism," which is often the disparaging term for talent, has become a dirty word.

As for me, I have often thought of that Asheville summer of 1935 and Fitzgerald's warning. "Press agents," he said one evening, "are glorified pimps on expense accounts." But I needed a job and never regretted my days on the project. Like so many others in the press department I longed to write for myself; to turn the show prose into something more creative and lasting. But *The Lost Colony* led me to The Playwrights' Company on Broadway, national tours, and to San Francisco with the Civic Light Opera. A road that led me further away from *Contempo* and *Singing Piedmont,* a one-act play I had written after seeing the Harlem *Macbeth,* and which Alfred Kreymborg described as "a minor classic." It was only by quitting altogether and spending a long time in Europe to avoid tempting offers that I was able to return to the reporting and writing that I loved.

Fitzgerald was right about the lure of the Friday pay check and the "swindle sheet" expense account, but he was wrong about many of my colleagues from the Federal Theatre press department. Milton Meltzer wrote two dozen books and became a member of the Authors Guild Council. Sam Chavkin was a Latin-American correspondent before he published *The Mind Stealers.* Ted Mauntz worked with Daniel Schorr, and Max Shohet became news editor of the FCC in charge of foreign broadcasts from Washington. They all made the leap from "the daily stint" to the tougher, more exacting world of fiction and creative journalism.

I like to think that it was because we worked for a tough and brilliant lady. For a time Hallie Flanagan was one of the most important women in America. Along with Eleanor Roosevelt and Frances Perkins she shaped the lives, attitudes, and opinions of millions of our citizens. She was demanding and courageous and she believed that the theatre could be truly national and excellent at the same time. We all knew that her stands were controversial and that she wanted the project to strive for "a more dramatic statement and better understanding of the great forces of life." Hallie believed that the theatre was worthy as a civilizing force and that a free theatre was one of our greatest treasures. She fought that final battle because she believed the fight was crucial to us as a people. For, "the theatre," to give Hallie the final word, "when it is good, is always dangerous."

Acknowledgments

IN the preparation of this manuscript we have drawn upon my experiences in 1935–1939, when I was on the Federal Theatre Project of New York City, during which time I was a reporter for its magazine, editor of a projected history of the city project, and press representative for four of its major productions. My memory of events was refreshed and supplemented by the writings of Hallie Flanagan, particularly *Arena,* her personal history of the project, and *The Federal Theatre* by Jane Mathews from which I have quoted frequently and to which I am deeply indebted. We would also like to acknowledge John Houseman's *Run-Through* and Willson Whitman's *Bread and Circuses* as valuable sources in recreating the confusion and excitement of the project.

Additional information and material was provided by Professor Lorraine A. Brown and Mae Mallory Krulak of the Federal Theatre Research Center, George Mason University; Lorraine Carroll, new head of the Research Center, and Carol Jean Baxter, Special Collections at the Center, Leonard Rapport, of the National Archives in Washington; Frances Goudy, special collections library, Vassar College; and Mary B. Trott, assistant archivist, Smith College. We take this opportunity to thank them, with additional thanks to Professor Brown and Mrs. Krulak for supplying photo copies of, and sketches from, the *Federal Theatre Magazine,* and correspondence, press reports, etc., of project activities while I was on Federal Theatre, all of which are now in the research center files.

We also take this opportunity to thank Malcolm Cowley for suggesting that this memoir be written and for his continued interest until its final publication; Paul Green for his criticism of an early draft and for bringing the manuscript to the

Acknowledgments

attention of Editor Malcolm L. Call; Archibald MacLeish for his thoughtful reading of the manuscript; the late Don Freeman and his widow, Lydia Cooley Freeman, for permission to use his sketches, most of which appeared in the project magazine; the Margo Feiden Galleries which represent Freeman; Henry Senber for his help and encouragement with theatrical anecdotes of the period; and the late Lawrence Gellert and James T. Hughes for jogging my memory on events and supplying me with helpful information.

We also wish to thank, some of whom I worked with on the project, for material furnished via interviews, telephone, or letter: Howard Bay, Ivan Black, Hilda Tunic Berman, Samuel Chavkin, Howard da Silva, Zelda Dorfman, H. I. Fishel, Frank Goodman, Rosamond Gilder, Hedley Gordon Graham, Ethel Aaron Hauser, John Houseman, Hallie Jonas, Aglaia and Herman Kilb, George Kondolf, Kate Drain Lawson, Gertrude Robbins Leavin, James Light, Allan Meltzer, Milton Meltzer, Arthur Miller, Lawrence Morris, Carlton Moss, Earl Robinson, Amelia Romano, Eleanor Scherr Shively, Bernard Simon, Max Shohet, Anna Sokolow, Virgil Thomson, Jay Williams, and George Zorn. We are sorry to note that many of these people have passed away while the book was in progress, but are fortunate to have had their help.

Our thanks for supplying additional information and in helping to locate project people: Salvator Attanasio, Peggy Baker, Anne Baxter, Eric Bentley, Milena and V. J. Buttitta, Grace Chapman Carbone, Howard Clurman, Marc Connelly, Jonathan Daniels, Charles W. Dibbell, William Hogan, Eunice Healey, Laurie Johnston, Robert Jonas, Barney Josephson, Ruth Katz, Beverly Kelley, Mary Ann King, Waldemar Korzeniowsky, Eva LeGallienne, Gladys Larack, John Howard Lawson, Edwin Lester, Jerre Mangione, Dorothy Meyer, Hobe Morrison, Gregory Morton, William Ndini, Anna Neagoe, James D. Proctor, Francis Robinson, Daniel Schorr, Sanford Seeger, Samuel Selden, Richard Watts, Richard Weaver, Alan D. Williams, Jed Mattes, and Ingalill Hjelm, managing editor of the University of Pennsylvania Press.

Bibliography

Books

Baker, Carlos. *Ernest Hemingway.* New York: Scribners, 1969.
Bentley, Eric (ed.) *Thirty Years of Treason.* New York: Viking, 1971.
Clurman, Harold. *The Fervent Years.* New York: Knopf, 1945.
Engel, Lehman. *This Bright Day.* New York: Macmillan, 1974.
Flanagan, Hallie. *Arena.* New York: Duell, Sloan and Pearce, 1940.
Flanagan, Hallie. *Dynamo.* New York: Duell, Sloan and Pearce, 1943.
Flanagan, Hallie. *Shifting Scenes.* New York: Coward-McCann, 1928.
Gaver, Jack. *Curtain Calls.* New York: Dodd Mead, 1947.
Goldstein, Malcolm. *The Political Stage.* New York: Oxford, 1974.
Himelstein, Morgan. *Drama Was a Weapon.* Rutgers, 1963.
Houseman, John. *Run-Through.* New York: Simon and Shuster, 1972.
Kronenberger, Louis. *Company Manners.* New York: Bobbs-Merrill, 1953.
Ludington, Townsend (ed.) *The Fourteenth Chronicle.* Boston: Gambit, 1973.
Mangione, Jerre. *The Dream and the Deal.* Boston: Little, Brown, 1972.
Mathews, Jane DeHart. *The Federal Theatre.* Princeton, 1967.
Meltzer, Milton. *Violins and Shovels.* New York: Delacorte, 1976.
O'Connor, John and Brown, Lorraine (eds.) *Free, Adult, Uncensored.* Washington: New Republic, 1978.
Schorer, Mark. *Sinclair Lewis.* New York: McGraw-Hill, 1961.
Taylor, Karen Malpede. *People's Theatre in Amerika.* New York: Drama Book Specialists, 1972.
Thomson, Virgil. *Virgil Thomson.* New York: Knopf, 1967.
Whitman, Willson. *Bread and Circuses.* New York: Oxford, 1937.
Williams, Jay. *Stage Left.* New York: Scribners, 1974.

Bibliography

Newspapers

New York Daily News. 1936–1939.

New York Journal American. 1935–1936.

New York Herald Tribune. 1935–1939.

New York Post. 1936–1939

New York Sun. 1936–1939.

New York Times. 1934–1939.

Variety. 1935–1939.

Magazines

Federal Theatre Bulletin. 1935.

New Theatre Magazine. 1935–1937.

Federal Theatre Magazine. 1935–1937.

The Nation. 1936–1939.

New Republic. 1935–1939.

Stage. 1937.

Theatre Arts Monthly. 1935–1939

Theatre Arts Committee Magazine. 1937–1938.

Index

Index

Index

Index

Index

Index

248

Index